# sentence composing for ELEMENTARY school

## A WORKTEXT TO BUILD BETTER SENTENCES

DON and JENNY KILLGALLON

2000

HEINEMANN
Portsmouth, NH

**Heinemann**
A division of Reed Elsevier Inc.
361 Hanover Street
Portsmouth, NH 03801–3912
www.heinemann.com

*Offices and agents throughout the world*

**Library of Congress Cataloging-in-Publication Data**
Killgallon, Don.
    Sentence composing for elementary school : a worktext to build better sentences /
Don and Jenny Killgallon.
        p.   cm.
    Includes bibliographical references.
    ISBN 0-325-00223-1
    1. English language—Sentences—Study and teaching (Elementary).   2. English
language—Composition and exercises—Study and teaching (Elementary).   I. Killgallon,
Jenny.   II. Title.
    LB1576.K483   2000
    372.62'3—dc21                                                                    99–053185

*Editor: Ray Coutu*
*Production: Elizabeth Valway*
*Cover design: Jenny Jensen Greenleaf*
*Manufacturing: Louise Richardson*

Printed in the United States of America on acid-free paper
04   03   02   01   00   VG   1   2   3   4   5

# Contents

# Contents

*To children everywhere:*
*Kylie, Brennan, Teagan,*
*and all the "grands" to come,*
*all the generations*
*to follow*

"The best [textbook on sentence improvement] appears to be the Killgallon series" (Evans 1987, 9). This comment came from the Canadian Ministry of Education after a two-year research project in which various textbooks on sentence improvement were piloted. Now, four worktexts on sentence composing—for elementary school, middle school, high school, and college—are available from Boynton/Cook, Heinemann for use on any level wherever writing is taught.

*Sentence Composing for Elementary School*, the latest in the series, is based upon imitation—in the conviction that students learn to write better sentences by imitating better sentences. For that reason, only professionally written sentences, many taken from literature read in the intermediate grades in elementary school, are used as models for students to imitate.

In addition to serving as models for better composing, the exclusive use of professionally written model sentences from widely read preteen literature provides intensive practice in interpreting of sentences. The recurring techniques of chunking, unscrambling, combining, expanding, and imitating require careful reading of authors' sentences, so the many practices enhance students' reading ability.

Many model sentences for *Sentence Composing for Elementary School* were chosen from novels and short stories from these lists of highly regarded preteen literature:

- Newberry Award or Honor books, an annual list of the best children's books published each year.

- *New York Times Review of Books*: "Reader's Catalog of Titles of Books for Young Readers—Eights, Nines, and Up." This list presents 639 titles arranged in best-selling order. (*Where the Wild Things Are* is No. 1.)

- National Education Association's list of the 100 titles most frequently recommended by teachers of the elementary grades. (*Charlotte's Web* is No. 1, and therefore the exclusive source for the review practices on pages 114–23.)

From these and other sources—from *Charlotte's Web* to *Harry Potter*—titles recommended for preteens were reviewed to select model sentences used in *Sentence Composing for Elementary School*. With those model sentences, students learn to imitate the way authors use various skills in their writing. The first section of this worktext (Learning Sentence Imitating) provides practice in sentence imitating to teach students the imitating process used throughout the rest of the worktext.

Throughout *Sentence Composing for Elementary School*, practices use five sentence composing techniques: chunking, unscrambling, combining, expanding, and imitating. Students use these techniques to learn how authors use certain skills. For each skill, there are seven practices. After the practices, two applications require students to use the skill in their own writing: one application for sentences, one for a paragraph. Finally, the review at the end of the worktext teaches students how to use the skills in combination within the same sentence.

The skills covered represent the kind of grammatical skills typically taught in the intermediate grades; however, the treatment in *Sentence Composing for Elementary School* is atypical because students see how authors use the skills and learn to imitate them. Imitating better sentences leads to writing better sentences.

As a result of the sentence composing worktext series, the sentence composing approach to writing improvement is widely used in innovative classrooms on all levels—elementary, middle, and high schools and college. The theoretical and historical background of the approach is detailed in *Sentence Composing: The Theory Booklet* (1998), available separately from Boynton/Cook, Heinemann. Here are some excerpts relevant to elementary school.

## Sentence Composing: A New Rhetoric

In his *Notes Toward a New Rhetoric*, Francis Christensen (1967) said, "I want them [students] to become sentence acrobats, to dazzle by their syntactic dexterity. I'd rather have to deal with hyperemia than anemia" (137). Sentence composing provides necessary and sufficient acrobatic training. All four sentence composing techniques—unscrambling, imitating, combining, expanding—use literature as a school for writing with a faculty of professional writers. The course the faculty brilliantly teaches is crucial to students' success as writers: what Christensen called "syntactic dexterity."

Also in his *Notes Toward a New Rhetoric*, Christensen advocated an integration of literature, writing, and grammar: "What I am proposing," he claimed, "carries over of itself into the study of literature. It makes the student *a better reader* of literature *[emphasis added]*. It helps him thread the syntactical mazes of much mature writing. . . ." (137). Through sentence composing activities, students increase their understanding of, and consequent skill in, both literature and writing.

In the past, teachers have neglected the sentence as a way to teach writing, using sentences instead as specimens for dissection, not as models for imitation. Only paragraphs, essays, or stories were used as models. After reading those longer models, students were told by their teachers, "Go, thou, and do likewise." Utterly unbreachable, the gap between the long professional model and the student's grasp of it was too wide, and so students were doomed to fall. The reach far exceeded the grasp.

With sentence composing, the gap sharply narrows because the model is graspable: it is only *one sentence long*. Students here, too, are told, "Go, thou, and do likewise." But this time they succeed, often amazingly, students ranging from our most challenged to our most challenging. Here, with only a *single sentence* as the model, and with frequent imitation activities through the four sentence composing techniques, students succeed.

In the past, the sentence was used as an object of analysis, resulting in literary paralysis. Sentence composing reverses the order, on the assumption that "doing" results in "knowing," that imitation leads to acquisition.

Much of the sentence composing approach owes a debt to the pioneering linguist Francis Christensen (1967), the first to see the light, who wrote in *Notes Toward a New Rhetoric*, "If the new grammar is to be brought to bear on composition, it must be brought to bear on the rhetoric of the sentence. . . . With hundreds of handbooks and rhetorics to draw from I have never been able to work out a program for teaching the sentence as I find it in the work of contemporary writers" (129).

Francis Christensen's life's work inspired sentence composing, "a program for teaching the sentence as [it is found] in the work of contemporary writers."

The foundation of the sentence composing approach is imitation. Everybody knows that a baby learns to talk partly by imitating the sentences of people who know how to talk. Every teacher of writing needs to know that a student can learn to write partly by imitating the sentences of good writers.

Imitation is both sincere flattery, and profound pedagogy. With the sentence composing approach, students imitate the masters of the art of writing. Our job—and yours—is to show them how.

—Don and Jenny Killgallon
Baltimore, Maryland

**References**

*Citations:*

Christensen, F. 1967. *Notes Toward a New Rhetoric.* New York: Harper & Row Publishers, Inc.

Evans, P., ed. 1987. *Beyond the ands and buts: Sentence Combining Resources for Integrated Programs, Grades 8–12, English and Anglais.* Toronto, Ontario: Ontario Institute for Studies in Education (OISE) Press.

**Sentence Composing Series**

*Worktexts:*

Killgallon, D., 1997. *Sentence Composing for Middle School.* Portsmouth, NH: Boynton/Cook Publishers.

———. 1998. *Sentence Composing for High School.* Portsmouth, NH: Boynton/Cook Publishers.

———. 1998. *Sentence Composing for College.* Portsmouth, NH: Boynton/Cook Publishers.

Killgallon, D., and J. Killgallon. 2000. *Sentence Composing for Elementary School.* Portsmouth, NH: Heinemann.

*History and Theory:*

Killgallon, D. 1998. *Sentence Composing: The Theory Booklet.* Portsmouth, NH: Boynton/Cook Publishers.

Imitation is a good way to learn—at any age. When you first started to walk, you probably imitated your parents. When you first learned to talk, chances are your parents pronounced the words, and you attempted to imitate the same sounds. In learning to walk and to talk, you used models to learn.

Think for a minute about things you learned by imitating people. How about these? What other activities did you learn by imitating?

| | |
|---|---|
| Playing a sport | Making a sandwich |
| Operating a computer | Riding a bike |
| Playing an instrument | Using a new slang expression |
| Learning a hobby | Changing a diaper |

Your goal in this worktext, *Sentence Composing for Elementary School*, is to learn how to compose better sentences by imitating model sentences by real authors. Model sentences in this worktext come from a literary treasure chest:

- books honored with awards;
- classics loved by every generation;
- novels studied by students your age in schools; and
- favorites enjoyed by young people.

Throughout this worktext, you will learn how to write sentences like the sentences of authors. Underneath each model sentence look for the title and the author.

You will practice using the tools authors use to build their sentences. Imitating how authors skillfully use those tools can help you to become a better writer. When you carefully finish the many practices in this book, you will have a "writer's toolbox" to use to build better sentences.

sentence
composing for
ELEMENTARY
school

# Practice 1: Chunking

People read and write sentences one sentence part at a time. Each sentence part is a "chunk" of meaning in the sentence.

1. Read each pair of sentences a chunk (sentence part) at a time.

2. Copy the sentence that makes sense because it is divided into meaningful chunks.

**EXAMPLE** ——————————————————————————————

**Sentences:**

a. The / idea of cutting and sewing a / dress by / herself was novel and exciting.

b. The idea / of cutting and sewing a dress / by herself / was novel and exciting.

Elizabeth George Speare, The Witch of Blackbird Pond

**Correct: b**

1a. They walked into / the bull / ring in the bright daylight of five / o'clock.

1b. They walked / into the bull ring / in the bright daylight / of five o'clock.

Maia Wojciechowska, *Shadow of a Bull*

2a. Sixteen children / and young people / were stricken with the mysterious fever, / and none of the familiar remedies / seemed to be of any benefit.

2b. Sixteen children and young / people were stricken with the mysterious / fever, and none of the familiar / remedies seemed to be of any / benefit.

Elizabeth George Speare, *The Witch of Blackbird Pond*

3a. The next day after / school, Jess went down and got the lumber he / needed, carrying it a couple of / boards at a time to the / creek bank.

3b. The next day after school, / Jess went down / and got the lumber he needed, / carrying it a couple of boards at a time / to the creek bank.

Katherine Paterson, *Bridge to Terabithia*

4a. When the / people in Central / Park learned that one of / the toy sailboats was being steered by a mouse in / a sailor suit, they / all came running.

4b. When the people / in Central Park / learned that one of the toy sailboats / was being steered by a mouse / in a sailor suit, / they all came running.

E. B. White, *Stuart Little*

5a. I saw / a gray-green slimy thing / like a snail / without its shell, / only bigger, / the size of a rat.

5b. I saw a / gray-green slimy / thing like a snail without / its shell, only / bigger, the / size of a rat.

K. A. Applegate, *Animorphs: The Invasion*

# Practice 2: Chunking to Imitate

1. The slash marks (/) in the model divide the sentence into chunks.

2. Copy and divide the imitation sentence into the same chunks.

**EXAMPLE** ──────────────────────────────────────────

**Model:**

Harriet started, / very slowly, / heart pounding, / to pull the ropes of the dumbwaiter / that would start her downward.

Louise Fitzhugh, Harriet the Spy

**Imitation:**

Jackson walked, / most confidently, / smile spreading, / to receive the award for the spelling contest / that had challenged the contestants constantly.

1a. MODEL: Then he turned / and stood still, / with the sun at his back, / and studied the water again.

Gary Paulsen, *Hatchet*

1b. IMITATION: Now Harriet nodded and became interested, with the Internet on her screen, and examined the web site thoroughly.

2a. MODEL: Pieces of tree, / pieces of metal, / pieces of seat and airplane wing / gleamed in the moonlight.

Caroline B. Cooney, *Flight #116 Is Down*

2b. IMITATION: Stories of courage, stories of suspense, stories of adventure and romance remained in the child's memory.

3a. MODEL: Crossing the lawn that morning, / Douglas Spaulding / broke a spider web with his face / when a single invisible line on the air / touched his brow / and snapped without a sound.

Ray Bradbury, *Dandelion Wine*

3b. IMITATION: Frying his body all day, Jacob Johnson got a horrible sunburn by afternoon because the cheap suntan lotion from his brother became a thin liquid and dripped into the sand.

4a. MODEL: Every sort of animal, / from bears to black beetles, / came sporting or shambling or scurrying / along their way, / and the high sky / that had been as sandy and arid as the soil itself, / now blossomed with birds.

Peter S. Beagle, *The Last Unicorn*

4b. IMITATION: All kinds of vegetables, from celery to fresh tomatoes, were laughing or dancing or playing in the salad bowl, and the salad dressing that had been as quiet and unnoticed as the bowl itself, suddenly giggled with glee.

# Practice 3: Chunking to Imitate

1. Copy the model sentence.

2. Copy the only sentence in the pair underneath the model that imitates the model.

3. Draw slash marks (/) to show the chunks like the ones in the model.

## EXAMPLE

**Model:**

He was in the bushes in moments, / scattering the birds, / grabbing branches, / stripping them to fill his mouth with berries.

Gary Paulsen, Hatchet

**Sentences:**

a. The firemen ran up the stairwell, entered the third floor to evacuate the apartments, and directed people to the safest exit.

b. Dad was on the riding mower in the afternoon, cutting the grass, bagging clippings, mulching them to cover his plantings for protection.

**Chunks Like Model: b**

Dad was on the riding mower in the afternoon, / cutting the grass, / bagging clippings, / mulching them to cover his plantings for protection.

MODEL ONE: With Miss Turner's map, / I found the first stone wall / that marked the farm.

Jean Craighead George, *My Side of the Mountain*

1a. In the final inning, Juan caught the home run ball that won the game.

1b. After the alarm was turned off, he got up and went to get ready for school.

MODEL TWO: The head was ugly, / a slag heap of melted-looking, / black pebbled skin.

K. A. Applegate, *Animorphs: The Attack*

2a. Ahead the road curved, turning very suddenly and dangerously, almost like the letter *u*.

2b. Our discovery was amazing, a treasure chest of expensive-appearing, golden dazzling jewels.

MODEL THREE: The fox coughed, / gagged, / and sneezed, / and the Stinky Cheese Man / flew off his back / and into the river, / where he fell apart.

Jon Scieszka, "The Stinky Cheese Man"

3a. A droid slid, bent, and fell, and the Jedi warrior climbed down the hill and into the desert, where the droid lay broken.

3b. The jungle was dark, dense, and scary, but Tarzan, near the waterfall in the rain forest, swung from the vines to save the gorillas.

# Practice 4: Unscrambling to Imitate

1. Unscramble both lists of sentence parts to imitate the same model.

2. Imitate the arrangement of sentence parts in the model.

**EXAMPLE**

**Model to Imitate:**

There was water to draw and linen to scrub, and, everlastingly, the endless rows of vegetables to weed and hoe.

Elizabeth George Speare, The Witch of Blackbird Pond

**Lists:**

a. and trash to haul

b. and, especially the weekly list of chores to start and complete

c. there was grass to mow


a. and games to play

b. and, always, the exciting seasonal sports to play and enjoy

c. there was music to hear

**Imitations:**

There was grass to mow and trash to haul, and, especially, the weekly list of chores to start and complete.


There was music to hear and games to play, and, always, the exciting seasonal sports to play and enjoy.

FIRST MODEL: When a child loves you / for a long, long time, / you become real.

Margery Williams, *The Velveteen Rabbit*

1a.  gave the forecast for blue, blue skies

1b.  the weather turned nasty

1c.  while the weatherman

2a.  the gorillas became worried

2b.  as the tiger

2c.  chased Tarzan with fast, fast, strides

SECOND MODEL: When the bell rang for recess, / he put on his red jacket / and walked outside, / alone.

Louis Sachar, *There's a Boy in the Girl's Bathroom*

3a.  delighted

3b.  after the daffodils appeared in spring

3c.  and worked outdoors

3d.  Grandma got out her gardening tools

4a.  and went downstairs

4b.  because the puppy whimpered at night

4c.  concerned

4d.  Sandy rose from the bed

# Practice 5: Unscrambling and Imitating

1. Unscramble the list of sentence parts to imitate the model.

2. Write your own imitation of the model.

**EXAMPLE** ───────────────────────────────

**Model to Imitate:**

While everyone scattered, I crept into my favorite hiding place, the little closet tucked under the stairs.

Jean Fritz, Homesick: My Own Story

**Scrambled Sentence Parts:**

a. a temporary tent made from a cardboard box

b. Levar came out from the shelter

c. when the rain ended

**Unscrambled Sentence:**

When the rain ended, Levar came out from the shelter, a temporary tent made from a cardboard box.

**Sample Imitation:**

After the light changed, the bus arrived at everybody's favorite restaurant, a huge building packed with hungry tourists.

1. MODEL: Four dolphins, swimming side by side, were pushing the raft through the water.

    Arthur C. Clarke, *Dolphin Island*

    a. were playing tug-of-war with a banana

    b. tumbling over each other

    c. baby chimpanzees

2. MODEL: They parted the bushes on the bank and peered out over the water.

    Mark Twain, *The Adventures of Tom Sawyer*

    a. and raced back toward the starting gate

    b. rounded the corner of the track

    c. the horses

3. MODEL: The third girl, holding her own mirror, used an eyebrow pencil to give herself a heavy brow.

    Beverly Cleary, *Ramona and Her Father*

    a. used the tractor to give the soil a good tilling

    b. renewing the school's agricultural field

    c. the high school students

4. MODEL: Alan and Tom and Joe leaned on their shovels under a tree in the apple orchard, watching the worms they had dug squirming on a flat rock.

    Thomas Rockwell, *How to Eat Fried Worms*

    a. in the frightful land of Dorothy's imagination

    b. prowling the territory they had traveled searching for a fresh victim

    c. lions and tigers and bears roamed through the forest

# Practice 6: Combining to Imitate

1. Combine both lists of sentences to imitate the same model.

2. Change the first sentence into the first sentence part of the model, change the second sentence into the second sentence part of the model, etc.

## EXAMPLE

**Model to Imitate:**

She loved to stroke the little pig, to feed him, to put him to bed.

E. B. White, *Charlotte's Web*

**Lists:**

a. Natalie wanted to do several things.

b. She wanted to conduct scientific experiments.

c. She wanted to learn physics.

d. She wanted to put science to work.

**Imitations:**

Natalie wanted to conduct scientific experiments, to learn physics, to put science to work.

a. Wilson liked to do several things.

b. He liked to plant the garden.

c. He liked to remove each new weed.

d. He liked to have soil to till.

Wilson liked to plant the garden, to remove each new weed, to have soil to till.

FIRST MODEL: He had some mouthwash, horrible stuff his mother made him gargle with when he had a cold.

Lynne Reid Banks, The Return of the Indian

1a. She had a jump rope.

1b. It was an exercise tool her doctor wanted her to use.

1c. The doctor wanted her to use it when she was strengthening her legs.

2a. Ralph had one brother.

2b. The brother was a neat kid Ralph's friends liked.

2c. Ralph's friends liked the brother when they played baseball.

SECOND MODEL: Once upon a time in a house by the sea lay an old woman, a special old woman who had the gift of magic.

Lois Duncan, A Gift of Magic

3a. Hidden in a cave near the castle on the mountain was a crystal ball.

3b. The crystal ball was a remarkable crystal ball.

3c. It was a crystal ball which showed a fantasy world in color.

4a. Once at the beach by our house on the cliff appeared a surfer.

4b. The surfer was an amazingly old surfer.

4c. The surfer was one who had a touch of eternal youth.

## Practice 7: Combining and Imitating

1. Combine the list of sentences to imitate the model.

2. Write your own imitation of the model.

**EXAMPLE** ───────────────────────────────────

**Model to Imitate:**

There they stood in their roomy ox stalls, clean and sleek and gleaming brown, with long black manes and tails.

Laura Ingalls Wilder, Farmer Boy

**Sentences to Combine:**

a. There they danced in the large multi-purpose room.

b. They were young and nervous but very excited.

c. They were with new pretty shirts and dresses.

**Combination:**

There they danced in the large multi-purpose room, young and nervous but very excited, with new pretty shirts and dresses.

**Sample Imitation:**

Soon the stars appeared in the huge theater lobby, glamorous and dashing and super confident, with constant perky smiles and laughter.

© 2000 by Don and Jenny Killgallon from *Sentence Composing for Elementary School*. Portsmouth, NH: Heinemann.

1. MODEL: Because he was so small, Stuart was often hard to find around the house.

E. B. White, *Stuart Little*

a. It happened when the train was very late.

b. Then passengers were usually easy to spot.

c. They could be spotted in the restaurant.

2. MODEL: Outside, the lights of towns and villages flickered in the distance as the Polar Express raced northward.

Chris Van Allsburg, *The Polar Express*

a. It happened nearby.

b. The exhibits of computers and printers filled with crowds.

c. This happened because the sale prices lowered further.

3. MODEL: The king gripped the arms of his chair, closed his eyes, clenched his teeth, and sweated.

T. H. White, *Book of Merlyn*

a. Our dog dragged a big bone in its jaws.

b. It jumped the little fence.

c. It dropped the bone.

d. And it panted.

4. MODEL:  From the earliest times, rats lived around the edges of human cities and farms, stowed away on men's ships, gnawed holes in their floors and stole their food.

Robert C. O'Brien, *Mrs. Frisby and the Rats of NIMH*

a. It happened in the warm seashore air.

b. Seagulls flocked toward the food of wasteful residents and tourists.

c. They lunched on leftovers on beaches.

d. They picked crumbs from the sand.

e. And they ate garbage.

## Activity 1: Sentences

1. Write imitations of each model.

2. Exchange papers with a partner and see if you and your partner can guess each other's models.

### MODELS

1. Again and again they could see the sea from the windows.

   > Lois Lowry, *Number the Stars*

2. His voice, cracked but triumphant, shattered the dead air.

   > Armstrong Sperry, *Call It Courage*

3. He was awake, jerked suddenly into consciousness in the black stillness of the night.

   > Katherine Paterson, *Bridge to Terabithia*

### EXAMPLES OF IMITATIONS

(Guess the models:)

1. The doctor was asleep, phoned unexpectedly by the hospital for emergency surgery on an accident victim.

2. Over and over they would ride the roller coaster for excitement.

3. The cement truck, noisy and gigantic, poured the fresh concrete.

## Activity 2: Paragraphs

1. Read the description in the model paragraph of a miniature imaginary horse inside a cupboard.

2. Study the sample imitation paragraph, one sentence at a time. Notice how the sentences in the imitation paragraph are written like the sentences in the model paragraph.

3. Write your own paragraph describing any real or imaginary animal, imitating the way the sentences are written in both the model and imitation paragraphs.

**MODEL PARAGRAPH** ——————————————————————————

(1) There, inside the cupboard, prancing and pawing the white paint, was a lovely, shiny-coated little brown horse. (2) As the cupboard door swung open, the horse shied nervously, turning his face and pricking his ears. (3) Its tiny nostrils flared, and its black tail plumed above his haunches as it gave a high, shrill neigh.

Lynne Reid Banks, *The Indian in the Cupboard*

**SAMPLE IMITATION PARAGRAPH** ——————————————————————

(1) Now, within the park, racing and chasing the bouncing ball, was the little, black-haired fast Happy-Dog. (2) When the ball stopped suddenly, Happy-Dog stopped immediately, making a u-turn and heading for it. (3) His movement slowed, and his two front paws raised above the ball as his owner yelled a cheerful, praising comment.

## Practice 1: Matching

Prepositional phrases begin with short words like these: *about, at, to, with, for, in, around, like, beyond, from, off, along, near, inside, outside, by, on, at, upon, down, up, inside, outside, over, under, through*. These words and other prepositions will fit into this blank: IT WAS _____ THE TREE.

    Use commas for prepositional phrases that describe a person, place, or thing, but no commas for phrases that identify a person, place, or thing. Most phrases in this worktext describe, so commas are needed.

    Prepositional phrases occur at the beginning of a sentence (*opener*), between a subject and verb (*s-v split*), or at the end of a sentence (*closer*).

    Most prepositional phrases end with a noun as in the examples: *wolf, coat, quarterdeck, home, rabbits.*

### EXAMPLES OF PREPOSITIONAL PHRASES ────────────────────

(Note: Frequently prepositional phrases occur in different places, or in a row)

Opener: <u>Like a lean, gray wolf</u>, he moved silently and easily.

> Joan Aiken, *A Necklace of Raindrops*

S-V Split: Captain Eaton, <u>in his good blue coat</u>, was shouting orders from the quarterdeck. (Also <u>from the quarterdeck</u>)

> Elizabeth George Speare, *The Witch of Blackbird Pond*

Closer: He was a Real Rabbit at last, <u>at home with</u> <u>the other rabbits</u>. (Two prepositional phrases in a row)

> Margery Williams, *The Velveteen Rabbit*

### Directions:

1. Match the prepositional phrases with the sentences.

2. Write out each sentence, inserting and underlining the prepositional phrase.

3. Use all three positions at least once—opener, subject-verb split, closer.

**Sentences:**

1. The horses pricked up their ears when they heard the goose hollering.

    E. B. White, *Charlotte's Web*

2. Pies were baking in the oven.

    Ray Bradbury, "I See You Never"

3. Their path wound, in and out.

    Lois Lenski, *Strawberry Girl*

4. He could see that the sun had melted into the horizon, but to the east the sky looked dark and bruised.

    Donna Hill, "Ghost Cat"

5. Jonas searched the auditorium for a glimpse of his father

    Lois Lowry, *The Giver*

6. I saw the three Sadler kids walking barefoot along the shore.

    R. L. Stine, *Ghost Beach*

**Prepositional Phrases:**

(Prepositions are <u>underlined</u>.)

a. <u>inside</u> Mrs. O'Brien's kitchen
   *(one prepositional phrase)*

b. <u>in</u> shorts and sleeveless T-shirts
   *(one prepositional phrase)*

c. <u>from</u> his place <u>in</u> the balcony
   *(two prepositional phrases in a row)*

d. <u>in</u> their stalls <u>in</u> the barn
   *(two prepositional phrases in a row)*

e. <u>to</u> the west, <u>through</u> the trees
   *(two prepositional phrases in a row)*

f. <u>through</u> the scrub, <u>around</u> palmetto clumps, <u>over</u> trunks <u>of</u> fallen trees, <u>under</u> dwarf pines and oaks
   *(many prepositional phrases in a row)*

# Practice 2: Identifying

1. Review what you learned about prepositional phrases in Practice 1. Jot down brief answers to these questions on a piece of your paper.

    a.  What information do prepositional phrases tell?

    b.  Are prepositional phrases sentences, or sentence parts?

    c.  What words usually begin prepositional phrases?

    d.  How long are prepositional phrases—short, medium, long?

    e.  Where can prepositional phrases be placed in a sentence?

    f.  When is one comma used for a prepositional phrase? Two commas?

    g.  How can prepositional phrases improve your writing?

2. Find the prepositional phrases in these sentences, and see if your answers fit them.

© 2000 by Don and Jenny Killgallon from *Sentence Composing for Elementary School*. Portsmouth, NH: Heinemann.

1.  With the flavor of ham and biscuit in his mouth, the boy felt good.

    William H. Armstrong, *Sounder*

2.  Over the river and through the woods, to Grandmother's house we go.

    Anonymous

3.  The curtains, like her bed cover, were faded and limp.

    Lynne Reid Banks, *One More River*

4.  In the moonlight, Sophie caught a glimpse of an enormous long wide wrinkly face with the most enormous ears.

    Roald Dahl, *The Big Friendly Giant*

5.  For two nights and days, imprisoned in his crate, Buck neither ate nor drank.

    Jack London, *The Call of the Wild*

6.  By the end of the class, Harry, like everyone else, was sweaty, aching, and covered in earth.

    J. K. Rowling, *Harry Potter and the Chamber of Secrets*

# Practice 3: Combining

1. Combine the two sentences by making the <u>underlined part</u> of the second sentence a prepositional phrase to put at the caret (^).

2. Write the new sentence and underline the prepositional phrase.

## EXAMPLE ——————————————————————————————————

**Sentences to Combine:**

a. The horses, ^, pricked up their ears when they heard the goose hollering.

b. The horses were <u>in their stalls in the barn</u>.

**Combination:**

The horses, <u>in their stalls in the barn</u>, pricked up their ears when they heard the goose hollering.

E.B. White, Charlotte's Web

1a.  ^ There was no sign that any other human being had ever been there.

1b.  It was <u>on the whole enormous prairie</u>.

Laura Ingalls Wilder, Little House on the Prairie

2a.  The Monster, ^, lunged forward with a terrible scream.

2b.  It lunged <u>at the first motion</u>.

Ray Bradbury, A Sound of Thunder

3a.  ^ The boy and the dog came to a small open space where there had once been a log ramp.

3b.  It was <u>in the pine woods, along a deserted logging road</u>.

William H. Armstrong, Sounder

4a.  ^ The boy had picked up the Indian by the waist between his thumb and forefinger.

4b.  He did it <u>with one quick movement</u>.

Lynne Reid Banks, The Indian in the Cupboard

5a.  Then they came, ^.

5b.  They came <u>up the street and around the house</u>.

Hal Borland, When the Legends Die

6a.  ^ The pig burst from under the fence, heaving Taran into the air.

6b.  It happened <u>in an explosion of dirt and pebbles</u>.

Lloyd Alexander, The Book of Three

## Practice 4: Unscrambling

1. Unscramble the list of sentence parts and write out the sentence.

2. Underline the sentence parts that are prepositional phrases. NOTE: The capitalized sentence part begins the sentence.

**EXAMPLE** ──────────────────────────────────────

**Scrambled Sentence Parts:**

a. upon the bats

b. On silent wings

c. the powerful bird swooped down

**Unscrambled Sentence:**

<u>On silent wings</u>, the powerful bird swooped down <u>upon the bats</u>.

Janell Cannon, *Stellaluna*

© 2000 by Don and Jenny Killgallon from *Sentence Composing for Elementary School*. Portsmouth, NH: Heinemann.

1a. and to know where to find them

1b. In a surprisingly short time

1c. he grew to recognize individual fish

                    Arthur C. Clarke, *Dolphin Island*

2a. filled

2b. On the way

2c. Claire's shoes

2d. with snow

2e. to school

                    Rosemary Wells, *First Tomato*

3a. dressed only

3b. In his dream

3c. he stood

3d. in his underwear

3e. of that very cafe

3f. in front

                    Chris Van Allsburg, *The Sweetest Fig*

4a. and dropped

4b. with a heavy jolt

4c. they hit the thick tree trunk

4d. to the ground

4e. With an earsplitting bang

4f. on wood

4g. of metal

                    J. K. Rowling, *Harry Potter and the Chamber of Secrets*

# Practice 5: Expanding

1. Create a prepositional phrase that begins with the words provided.
2. Vary the lengths of the prepositional phrases—some short, some medium, some long.

## EXAMPLE

**Sentence:**

At . . . , she raced Masakiro home and won easily.

**Sample Prepositional Phrases:**

Short:     At noon

Medium:   At the sound of the bell

Long:      At the last moment that she could

**Original Sentence:**

At the end of the day, she raced Masakiro home and won easily.

Eleanor Coerr, *Sadako and the Thousand Paper Cranes*

1. On . . . , there were mounds and mounds of walnuts, and the squirrels were working away like mad, shelling the walnuts at a tremendous speed.

    Roald Dahl, *Charlie and the Chocolate Factory*

2. The giant peach, with . . . , was like a massive golden ball sailing upon a silver sea.

    Roald Dahl, *James and the Giant Peach*

3. On . . . , the young prince appeared in Jemmy's chamber.

    Sid Fleischman, *The Whipping Boy*

4. The feast finished with an entertainment provided by . . .

    J. K. Rowling, *Harry Potter and the Prisoner of Azkaban*

5. On . . . , the people pressed forward, their faces strained to stillness as they watched Assateague Beach.

    Marguerite Henry, *Misty of Chincoteague*

6. Then, like . . . , he felt the comforting knowledge of wild creatures near.

    Alexander Key, *The Forgotten Door*

7. Through . . . , they watched their assorted clothing spill and splash over and over and around and around.

    E. L. Konigsburg, *From the Mixed-up Files of Mrs. Basil E. Frankweiler*

8. At . . . , she stood still and listened.

    Madeleine L'Engle, *A Wrinkle in Time*

9. With . . . , they struggled out of the thicket.

    C. S. Lewis, *Prince Caspian*

10. On . . . , they saw the Lion slowly walking away from them into the wood.

    C. S. Lewis, *The Lion, the Witch and the Wardrobe*

# Practice 6: Combining to Imitate

1. Combine both lists of sentences to imitate the same model.

2. Change the first sentence into the first sentence part of the model, and change the second sentence into the second sentence part of the model, etc.

## EXAMPLE

**Model to Imitate**

With a slight movement of his skinny fingers, he gestured the warriors to stand away.

Lloyd Alexander, The Book of Three

**Lists:**

a. It happened after the tenth practice of the new season.

b. Then the coach chose Jackson.

c. He chose Jackson to hit first.

**Imitations:**

After the tenth practice of the new season, the coach chose Jackson to hit first.

a. It occurred on the honeysuckle vine along the wooden fence.

b. There a hummingbird flapped its tiny wings.

c. It flapped them to feed furiously.

On the honeysuckle vine along the wooden fence, a hummingbird flapped its tiny wings to feed furiously.

FIRST MODEL: High against the pale clouds, seagulls soared and cried as if they were mourning.

Lois Lowry, *Number the Stars*

1a. It was right beside the closed door.

1b. The cat meowed and scratched.

1c. It was as if it were frightened.


2a. It happened just outside the darkened classroom.

2b. Children scampered and played.

2c. It was as if they were vacationing.

SECOND MODEL: Within the folds of his tunic, Tarik wiped his hands and placed his fingers around the handle of his sword.

Walter Dean Myers, *Legend of Tarik*

3a It was around the edges of the garden.

3b. They created a border.

3c. And planted flowers along the row of day lilies.


4a. It was on the top of his dresser.

4b. Jake placed his trophy.

4c. And remembered his victory against the boy from his school.

# Practice 7: Combining and Imitating

1. Combine each list of sentences to imitate the model.

2. Write your own imitation of the model.

## EXAMPLE

**Model to Imitate:**

Beside the hedgerow, she met Straw, the horse who was in pain from a toothache.

Roger Duvoisin, Petunia

**Sentences to Combine:**

a. It happened inside the bleachers.

b. A fan caught the ball.

c. The ball was the one that was from the star batter of the team.

**Combination:**

Inside the bleachers, a fan caught the ball, the one that was from the star batter of the team.

**Sample Imitation:**

During the song, the crowd cheered the guitarist, the one who was in the spotlight on the stage.

1. MODEL: In the middle of the last cookie, an inspiration came to her.

   Katherine Paterson, *The Great Gilly Hopkins*

   a. It was after the end of the birthday party.

   b. Another present arrived at her house.

2. MODEL: On this mound, among the grasses and the plants, stood Rontu.

   Scott O'Dell, *Island of the Blue Dolphins*

   a. It was on the floor.

   b. It was beside the shoes and the socks.

   c. Sat the magazine.

3. MODEL: Across the stalk land, into the pine woods, into the climbing, brightening glow of the dawn, the boy followed the dog, whose anxious pace slowed from age as they went.

   William H. Armstrong, *Sounder*

   a. It was down the long hall.

   b. It was into the crowded room.

   c. It was into the snaking, twisting line for the tickets.

   d. The man brought his son, whose nervous anticipation bubbled over from excitement as they waited.

4. MODEL: The fire made him think of home, of food and warmth and company, of faces around the evening circle, of the drone of old men's voices, telling their endless tales of daring.

   Armstrong Sperry, *Call It Courage*

   a. The rain made her think of summer.

   b. It made her think of grass and honeysuckle and tomatoes.

   c. It made her think of flowers in her backyard garden.

   d. It made her think of the chirp of nesting birds' voices, singing their lovely songs of the season.

## Activity 1: Sentences

1.  Write three sentences about unusual people, places, or things.

2.  Use at least one of each of the three kinds of prepositional phrases below, which are taken from the earlier practices.

**EXAMPLES OF KINDS OF PREPOSITIONAL PHRASES** ———————————

1.  SINGLE:

    a.  <u>inside</u> Mrs. O'Brien's kitchen
    b.  <u>in</u> shorts and sleeveless T-shirts
    c.  <u>in</u> the moonlight
    d.  <u>for</u> two nights and days
    e.  <u>with</u> one quick movement
    f.  <u>in</u> a surprisingly short time

2.  CONSECUTIVE:

    a.  <u>from</u> his place <u>in</u> the balcony
    b.  <u>on the way</u> <u>to</u> school
    c.  <u>at</u> the end <u>of</u> the day
    d.  <u>with</u> a slight movement <u>of</u> his skinny fingers
    e.  <u>after</u> the tenth practice <u>of</u> the new season
    f.  <u>on</u> the honeysuckle vine <u>along</u> the wooden fence

3.  SERIES: (connected by commas or the word *and*)

    a.  <u>over</u> the river and <u>through</u> the woods
    b.  <u>up</u> the street and <u>around</u> the house
    c.  <u>through</u> the scrub, <u>around</u> palmetto clumps, <u>over</u> trunks <u>of</u> fallen trees, <u>under</u> dwarf pines and oaks
    d.  <u>in</u> the pine woods, <u>along</u> a deserted logging road
    e.  <u>on</u> this mound, <u>among</u> the grasses and the plants

© 2000 by Don and Jenny Killgallon from *Sentence Composing for Elementary School*. Portsmouth, NH: Heinemann.

## Activity 2: Paragraphs

1. Write a paragraph describing a vacation.

2. Include <u>different kinds</u> of prepositional phrases in your paragraph: single, consecutive, series. (See examples on page 32.)

3. Use <u>different positions</u> for your prepositional phrases within your sentences. (See examples below.)

**EXAMPLES** ——————————————————————————————

1. Opener: <u>Like a lean, gray wolf</u>, he moved silently and easily.

   Joan Aiken, *A Necklace of Raindrops*

2. S-V Split: Captain Eaton, <u>in his good blue coat</u>, was shouting orders from the quarterdeck.

   Elizabeth George Speare, *The Witch of Blackbird Pond*

3. Closer: He was a Real Rabbit at last, <u>at home</u> <u>with the other rabbits</u>. (Two consecutive prepositional phrases)

   Margery Williams, *The Velveteen Rabbit*

# Practice 1: Matching

An appositive phrase is a sentence part that identifies a person, place, or thing named in a sentence. Appositives often begin with the words *a*, *an*, or *the*. They always answer one of these questions:

Who is he? Who is she? Who are they? *(people)*

What is it? *(place or thing)*

Appositives occur at the beginning of a sentence *(opener)*, between a subject and verb *(s-v split)*, or at the end of a sentence *(closer)*.

## EXAMPLES OF APPOSITIVES

Opener: <u>A professional individualist</u>, William T. Stead seemed almost to have planned his arrival.

> Walter Lord, *A Night to Remember*

S-V Split: Cotton, <u>the kitten</u>, went up the tree but could not come down.

> Roger Duvoisin, *Petunia*

Closer: May always liked the weird ones best, <u>the ones you couldn't peg right off</u>.

> Cynthia Rylant, *Missing May*

## Directions:

1. Match the appositives with the sentences.

2. Write out each sentence, inserting and underlining the appositive.

3. Use all three positions at least once—opener, s-v split, closer.

**Sentences:**

1. Nobody was around but Snowball.

   E. B. White, *Stuart Little*

2. One of the pups came slowly toward me.

   Scott O'Dell, *Island of the Blue Dolphins*

3. Andrew has made several bicycle tours through Europe.

   Andrew Kauser,
   "Challenging My Fears"

4. A tear trickled down his shabby velvet nose and fell to the ground.

   Margery Williams, *The Velveteen Rabbit*

5. It was a runt.

   Dick King-Smith, *Pigs Might Fly*

6. Inside was a small white metal cupboard with a mirror in the door.

   Lynne Reid Banks,
   *The Indian in the Cupboard*

**Appositives:**

a. a real tear

b. a round ball of fur that I could have held in my hand

c. an avid biker

d. the kind you see over the basin in old-fashioned bathrooms

e. the white cat belonging to Mrs. Little

f. a piglet born for some reason far smaller and weaker than its brothers and sisters

## Practice 2: Identifying

1. Review what you learned about appositives in Practice 1. Jot down brief answers to these questions on a piece of your paper.

   a. What information do appositives tell?

   b. Are appositives sentences, or sentence parts?

   c. What words usually begin appositives?

   d. How long are appositives—short, medium, long?

   e. Where can appositives be placed in a sentence?

   f. When is one comma used for an appositive? Two commas?

   g. How can appositives improve your writing?

2. Find the appositive phrases in these sentences, and see if your answers fit them.

1. This was a deer mouse, a little creature with big eyes and long hind legs like a miniature kangaroo.
   (HINT: What is a deer mouse?)

   Sheila Burnford, *The Incredible Journey*

2. Mike Mulligan had a steam shovel, a beautiful red steam shovel.
   (HINT: What is Mike's steam shovel?)

   Virginia Lee Burton, *Mike Mulligan and His Steam Shovel*

3. Earth, our little blue and green planet with the fluffy white clouds and all, is under attack.
   (HINT: What is earth? )

   K. A. Applegate, *Animorphs: The Underground*

4. On the fifth day, the day before Laurie's return to London, they went together to the riverbank.
   (HINT: What was the fifth day?)

   Phillippa Pearce, "Fresh"

5. Every year, Harry was left behind with Mrs. Figg, a mad old lady who lived two streets away.
   (HINT: Who was Mrs. Figg?)

   J. K. Rowling, *Harry Potter and the Sorcerer's Stone*

6. He remembered a chipmunk he had as a small boy, a pet that came when he called and ate in his hand.
   (HINT: What was the chipmunk?)

   Hal Borland, *When the Legends Die*

# Practice 3: Combining

1. Combine the two sentences by making the <u>underlined part</u> of the second sentence an appositive to put at the caret (^).

2. Write the new sentence and underline the appositive.

**EXAMPLE** ────────────────────────────────

**Sentences to Combine:**

a. The pilot seemed more a machine than a man, ^.

b. He seemed <u>an extension of the plane</u>.

**Combination:**

The pilot seemed more a machine than a man, <u>an extension of the plane</u>.

Gary Paulsen, Hatchet

1a. Moana, ^, was reaching up for them, seeking to draw them down to his dark heart.

1b. Moana was <u>the Sea God</u>.

> Armstrong Sperry, *Call It Courage*

2a. Curtis and Doug, ^, came out of Mrs. Sharp's class.

2b. They were <u>two of Jeff's friends</u>.

> Louis Sachar, *There's a Boy in the Girls' Bathroom*

3a. As far back as the 1960's, Dr. John Lilly, ^, had suggested ways in which they might cooperate with man.

3b. He was <u>the first scientist to attempt communication with dolphins</u>.

> Arthur C. Clarke, *Dolphin Island*

4a. Buck did not read the newspapers, and he did not know that Manuel, ^, was an undesirable acquaintance.

4b. Manuel was <u>one of the gardener's helpers</u>.

> Jack London, *The Call of the Wild*

5a. Grey damp would be around them, and the sun, ^, would fade away.

5b. The sun looked like <u>a copper penny</u>.

> T. H. White, *Book of Merlyn*

6a. The scrub, ^, was an unexplored wilderness, always beckoning the children.

6b. The scrub was <u>that big wild stretch of dry and sandy land where scrub oaks, scrub pines, and palmettos grew</u>.

> Lois Lenski, *Strawberry Girl*

# Practice 4: Unscrambling

1. Unscramble the list of sentence parts and write out the sentence.

2. Underline the sentence parts that are appositive phrases. NOTE: The capitalized sentence part begins the sentence.

---

**EXAMPLE**

**Scrambled Sentence Parts:**

a. Tobias

b. was about a hundred feet above us, floating on a nice warm current of air

c. the remaining member of our group

**Unscrambled Sentence:**

Tobias, <u>the remaining member of our group</u>, was about a hundred feet above us, floating on a nice warm current of air.

K. A. Applegate, *Animorphs: The Underground*

1a. was Cold Sassy's champion milk producer

1b. a tan Jersey named Blind Tillie

1c. One of them

> Olive Ann Burns, *Cold Sassy Tree*

2a. about me and Sheila

2b. the elevator operator

2c. Henry

2d. is always making jokes

> Judy Blume, *Tales of a Fourth Grade Nothing*

3a. just to dance

3b. a city far away from here

3c. Once they even went to St. Louis

> Joseph Krumgold, *And Now Miguel*

4a. The reason for this was that the toothpaste factory

4b. suddenly went bust and had to close down

4c. the place where Mr. Bucket worked

> Roald Dahl, *Charlie and the Chocolate Factory*

5a. the horse who was in pain from a toothache

5b. she met Straw

5c. Beside the hedgerow

> Roger Duvoisin, *Petunia*

6a. chose James

6b. She

6c. the second youngest of their three younger brothers

> E. L. Konigsburg, *From the Mixed-up Files of Mrs. Basil E. Frankweiler*

# Practice 5: Expanding

1. Create an appositive that begins with the words provided.

2. Vary the lengths of the appositives—some short, some medium, some long.

**EXAMPLE** ———————————————————————————————————

**Sentence:**

Another man came in, a man . . .

**Sample Appositives:**

Short:      a man about forty

Medium:   a man she had seen the other day

Long:       a man unable to stop yelling about his team's victory in the championship game

**Original Sentence:**

Another man came in, <u>a man in dusty Levis and a black hat mottled with sweat stains</u>.

Hal Borland, When the Legends Die

1. Wilbur planned to have a talk with Templeton, the rat. . . .

    E. B. White, *Charlotte's Web*

2. Once upon a time there was a bat, a little. . . .

    Randall Jarrell, "The Bat-Poet"

3. The ponies were scrambling up the beach, the long, sandy. . . .

    Marguerite Henry, *Misty of Chincoteague*

4. They all saw it this time, a whiskered. . . .

    C. S. Lewis, *The Lion, the Witch and the Wardrobe*

5. It was a pitiful sight, the three. . . .

    Cynthia Rylant, *Missing May*

6. Suddenly they were aware of someone coming toward them, a tall. . . .

    Rachel Field, *Calico Bush*

7. On the fifth day, the day . . . , they went together to the riverbank.

    Philippa Pearce, "Fresh"

8. He felt the young man's surge of joy at seeing his brother alive, the brother. . . .

    Madeleine L'Engle, *A Swiftly Tilting Planet*

9. Tom Grieves, the handyman who . . . , named the birds Peter Soil and Maggie Mess.

    Frank B. Gilbreth and Ernestine Gilbreth Carey, *Cheaper by the Dozen*

10. He came so close she could see on his head a few last straggly pinfeathers, the feathers. . . .

    Jean Craighead George, *The Fire Bug Connection*

# Practice 6: Unscrambling to Imitate

1. Unscramble both lists of sentence parts to imitate the same model.

2. Imitate the arrangement of sentence parts in the model.

## EXAMPLE

**Model to Imitate:**

A short round boy of seven, he took little interest in troublesome things, preferring to remain on good terms with everyone.

Mildred D. Taylor, *Roll of Thunder, Hear My Cry*

**Lists:**

a. a new enthusiastic teacher of math

b. wanting to teach with high interest for all her students

c. she taught most lessons with fun activities

a. the newest kid in the neighborhood

b. beginning to relate to all the other kids by sharing neat games

c. Lamont made friends with amazing speed

**Imitations:**

A new enthusiastic teacher of math, she taught lessons with fun activities, wanting to teach with high interest for all her students.

The newest kid in the neighborhood, Lamont made friends with amazing speed, beginning to relate to all the other kids by sharing neat games.

FIRST MODEL: John dusted off his best chair, a rocker with its runners off.

Joseph Krumgold, *Onion John*

1a. a fantasy

1b. her favorite book

1c. Susan picked up

1d. with incredible characters

2a. Mr. Short looked over

2b. of his son

2c. his current project

2d. a painting

SECOND MODEL: Mrs. Whatsit sighed, a sigh so sad that Meg wanted to put her arms around her and comfort her.

Madeleine L'Engle, *A Wrinkle in Time*

3a. to lift her and help her

3b. a stumble so awkward

3c. the child stumbled

3d. that her mother tried

4a. that the sky seemed

4b. a flash so bright

4c. the lightning flashed

4d. to light up the ground and frame it

# Practice 7: Unscrambling and Imitating

1. Unscramble the list of sentence parts to imitate the model.

2. Write your own imitation of the model.

**EXAMPLE** ————————————————————————————

**Model to Imitate:**

Sounder was making an awful noise, a half-strangled mixture of growl and bark.

William H. Armstrong, *Sounder*

**Scrambled Sentence Parts:**

a. of wire and wood

b. a flimsy barrier

c. the neighbor was inspecting the old fence

**Unscrambled Sentence:**

The neighbor was inspecting the old fence, a flimsy barrier of wire and wood.

**Sample Imitation:**

Jackson was mowing the overgrown lawn, the usual combination of grass and weeds.

1. MODEL: His eyes focused on Mama again, a tiny figure in the distance now.

Mildred D. Taylor, *Roll of Thunder, Hear My Cry*

a.  a fly ball in her area now

b.  the third base player

c.  followed the ball closely

2. MODEL: Gilly gave little William Ernest the most fearful face in all her repertory of scary looks, sort of a cross between Count Dracula and Godzilla.

Katherine Paterson, *The Great Gilly Hopkins*

a.  featured a new channel with lots of great movies

b.  pretty much an assortment of titles with action and suspense

c.  the cable company

3. The Trunchbull, this mighty female giant, stood there in her green breeches, quivering like a blancmange.

Roald Dahl, *Matilda*

a.  the baby

b.  walked around in her diapers, waddling like a duck

c.  a really frisky toddler

4. MODEL: He stood at the foot of the bridge that spanned the river, the bridge that citizens were allowed to cross only on official business.

Lois Lowry, *The Giver*

a.  only at discount prices

b.  that sold electronics products

c.  the mall where stores tried to sell things

d.  Angie went to the store in the mall

# Activity 1: Sentences

1. Write three sentences about famous people, real or imagined, living or dead.

2. Each sentence should contain an appositive phrase to identify the person.

3. Use each position—opener, s-v split, closer.

**EXAMPLES**

1. Opener: <u>The civil rights leader who fought for racial harmony</u>, Martin Luther King, Jr. inspired many people with his famous dream.

2. S-V Split: Elvis Presley, <u>the king of '50s rock and roll who achieved fame overnight</u>, made several appearances in big shows in Las Vegas.

3. Closer: Mickey Mouse is the most famous creation of Walt Disney, <u>the animated cartoon artist whose movies and theme parks are famous throughout the world</u>.

## Activity 2: Paragraphs

1. Write a paragraph of five to eight sentences describing your family or friends.

2. Start your paragraph with a topic sentence that pictures your family at a party or other celebration, or shows your friends at school or at play. Then describe what each person (family member or friend) is doing during the event.

3. Each sentence that names a person should contain an appositive phrase to identify the person.

4. Somewhere in your paragraph, use each position at least once—opener, s-v split, closer.

### EXAMPLES

1. Opener: <u>A short round boy of seven</u>, Christopher John took little interest in troublesome things, preferring to remain on good terms with everyone.

   Mildred D. Taylor, *Roll of Thunder, Hear My Cry*

2. S-V Split: Tobias, <u>the remaining member of our group</u>, was about a hundred feet above us, floating on a nice warm current of air.

   K. A. Applegate, *Animorphs: The Underground*

3. Closer: Out stepped Sam Beaver, <u>the boy who had visited them a month ago</u>.

   E. B. White, *The Trumpet of the Swan*

## Practice 1: Matching

A participial phrase is a sentence part that describes a person, place, or thing named in a sentence. Present participles always begin with a word that ends in *ing*. They always answer one of these questions:

What is he doing? What is she doing? What are they doing? *(people)*

What is it doing? *(place or thing)*

Participles occur at the beginning of a sentence *(opener)*, between a subject and verb (s-v split), or at the end of a sentence *(closer)*.

**EXAMPLES OF PARTICIPLES** ———————————————————

Opener: <u>Rising with the two pups held close to my chest</u>, I asked if I owned anything.

> Wilson Rawls, *Where the Red Fern Grows*

S- V Split: Sophie, <u>sitting on the Big Friendly Giant's hand</u>, peeped out of the cave.

> Roald Dahl, *The Big Friendly Giant*

Closer: She turned toward the window, <u>pressing her cheeks to the little glass panes to cool them of their smarting</u>.

> Rachel Field, *Calico Bush*

**Directions:**

1. Match the participles with the sentences.
2. Write out each sentence, inserting and underlining the participle.
3. Use all three positions at least once—opener, s-v split, closer.

# Using Participial Phrases

**Sentences:**

1. Suddenly the shark soared up out of the water in a fountain of spray.

   Willard Price, "The Killer Shark"

2. The children came charging back into their homeroom.

   Rosa Guy, *The Friends*

3. The ponies rolled in the wiry grass.

   Marguerite Henry, *Misty of Chincoteague*

4. The fly in the spider web was beating its wings furiously.

   E. B. White, *Charlotte's Web*

5. I closed my eyes again.

   Theodore Taylor, *The Cay*

6. I dream I'm flying over a sandy beach in the early morning.

   Toni Cade Bambara, *Raymond's Run*

**Participles:**

a. trying to break loose and free itself
b. letting out great whinnies of happiness
c. turning as it fell
d. touching the leaves of the trees as I fly by
e. thinking maybe I was dreaming
f. shouting and screaming

## Practice 2: Identifying

1.  Review what you learned about participial phrases in Practice 1. Jot down brief answers to these questions on a piece of your paper.

    a.  What information do participles tell?

    b.  Are participles sentences, or sentence parts?

    c.  Present participles end in what three letters?

    d.  How long are participles—short, medium, long?

    e.  Where can participles be placed in a sentence?

    f.  When is one comma used for a participle? Two commas?

    g.  How can participles improve your writing?

2.  Find the participial phrases in these sentences, and see if your answers fit them.

1. Arriving at the used-up haystack, the boy leaned against the barbed wire fence.

   John Steinbeck, *The Red Pony*

2. The snow swirled, blurring his vision.

   Lois Lowry, *The Giver*

3. A cloud shadow, drifting the breadth of Trial Valley, spread across the inscrutable face of Old Joshua.

   Bill and Vera Cleaver, *Where the Lilies Bloom*

4. Lying back in the soft hay, I folded my hands behind my head, closed my eyes, and let my mind wander back over the two long years.

   Wilson Rawls, *Where the Red Fern Grows*

5. Billy ate it offhand, sideways, reading a comic book.

   Thomas Rockwell, *How to Eat Fried Worms*

6. Returning to the lab to put a bucket of water on the stove for dish washing, she noticed that Mitch was not at the computer, although it was turned on.

   Jean Craighead George, *The Fire Bug Connection*

# Practice 3: Combining

1. Combine the two sentences by making the <u>underlined part</u> of the second sentence a participial phrase to put at the caret (^).

2. Write the new sentence and underline the participial phrase.

**Sentences to Combine:**

a. James stood alone, out in the open, ^.

b. He was <u>wondering what to do</u>.

**Combination:**

James stood alone, out in the open, <u>wondering what to do</u>.

Roald Dahl, *James and the Giant Peach*

1a. There is Sadako, ^.

1b. She is <u>standing on top of a granite mountain of paradise</u>.

Eleanor Coerr, Sadako and the Thousand Paper Cranes

2a. ^ The Trunchbull lowered him back into his chair beside the desk.

2b. She was <u>still holding him by the ears</u>.

Roald Dahl, Matilda

3a. He was standing very still, ^.

3b. He was <u>holding it tightly with both hands while the crowd pushed and shouted all around him</u>.

Roald Dahl, Charlie and the Chocolate Factory

4a. That afternoon, a big man came and pried off the drain cover, ^.

4b. He was <u>grunting as he worked</u>.

Pam Conrad, The Tub People

5a. She lay very still with her eyes closed, ^.

5b. She was <u>letting herself awaken slowly</u>.

Lois Duncan, A Gift of Magic

6a. ^ The prince breathed in the sweet, fresh air.

6b. He was <u>standing in the clear sunshine</u>.

Sid Fleischman, The Whipping Boy

# Practice 4: Unscrambling

1. Unscramble the list of sentence parts and write out the sentence.
2. Underline the sentence parts that are participial phrases. NOTE: The capitalized sentence part begins the sentence.

## EXAMPLE

**Scrambled Sentence Parts:**

a. at the edge of the field

b. sniffing the air currents

c. The doe paused

**Unscrambled Sentence:**

The doe paused at the edge of the field, <u>sniffing the air currents</u>.

Alexander Key, The Forgotten Door

1a. braced

1b. trying to tighten the grip of his legs about the unicorn's broad neck

1c. Charles Wallace

        Madeleine L'Engle, *A Swiftly Tilting Planet*


2a. stamping their bare feet on the floor to shake the sand off

2b. crowded in

2c. The children

        Lois Lenski, *Strawberry Girl*


3a. pressing her face in the feather bed to stifle her sobs

3b. Now when a buyer came to look at the colts

3c. Maureen did not run to her room as she used to do

        Marguerite Henry, *Misty of Chincoteague*


4a. rose and went out

4b. The White Witch

4c. ordering Edmund to go with her

        C. S. Lewis, *The Lion, the Witch and the Wardrobe*


5a. was watching this performance over the rim of her book with some interest

5b. Matilda

5c. nestling in her usual chair

        Roald Dahl, *Matilda*


6a. rolling over peaks and through valleys like a car on a roller coaster

6b. Faster and faster the Polar Express

6c. ran along

        Chris Van Allsburg, *The Polar Express*

## Practice 5: Expanding

1. Create a participial phrase that begins with the words provided.

2. Vary the lengths of the participial phrases—some short, some medium, some long.

**EXAMPLE** ————————————————————————

**Sentence:**

Fleet and Lee stood quietly side by side, watching. . . .

**Sample Participles:**

Short:      watching television

Medium:   watching the activity around the cafeteria

Long:       watching the interior decorators at the mall put up
              decorations that were created for the children's festival

**Original Sentence:**

Fleet and Lee stood quietly side by side, <u>watching the ice draw nearer</u>.

Walter Lord, A Night to Remember

1. As they swung on the turn, the sled went over, spilling. . . .

   Jack London, *The Call of the Wild*

2. Dad, sitting . . . , leaned forward so he could see.

   Phyllis Reynolds Naylor, *Shiloh*

3. Coming . . . , she could hear them talking in the room below, and she paused a moment to eavesdrop on their conversation.

   Robert C. O'Brien, *Mrs. Frisby and the Rats of NIMH*

4. The wind blew in fierce gusts as we left the village, stinging. . . .

   Scott O'Dell, *Island of the Blue Dolphins*

5. The next day after school, Jess went down and got the lumber he needed, carrying. . . .

   Katherine Paterson, *Bridge to Terabithia*

6. The sound came from the end of one corridor, and I fumbled along, peering. . . .

   Emily Neville, *It's Like This, Cat*

7. She just sat and stared out of the window, thinking. . . .

   E. B. White, *Charlotte's Web*

8. Sitting . . . , I could see that the covers of the books were badly worn.

   Mildred D. Taylor, *Roll of Thunder, Hear My Cry*

9. Ben got down on his hands and knees and eased his body over the edge of the cliff, slowing. . . .

   Robb White, *Deathwatch*

10. The frightening sound filled the forest, echoing. . . .

    R. L. Stine, *Ghost Beach*

# Practice 6: Combining to Imitate

1. Combine both lists of sentences to imitate the same model.

2. Change the first sentence into the first sentence part of the model and change the second sentence into the second sentence part of the model, etc.

## EXAMPLE

**Model to Imitate:**

The gulls circled and swooped, crying out in cold, hungry squawks.

Katherine Paterson, *Park's Quest*

**Lists:**

a. The children swam.

b. And the children giggled.

c. The children were leaping through waves in the summer surf.

a. The train slowed.

b. And the train stopped.

c. The train was screeching loudly from the responding brakes.

**Imitations:**

The children swam and giggled, leaping through waves in the summer surf.

The train slowed and stopped, screeching loudly from the responding brakes.

FIRST MODEL: He stood very straight and proud and unconcerned, holding the cape easily in his two hands.

Maia Wojciechowska, *Shadow of a Bull*

1a.  She waited very small and quiet and timid.

1b.  She was twisting the scarf nervously.

1c.  The scarf was on her lap.

2a.  He flew very high and straight and true.

2b.  He was moving swiftly.

2c.  He was moving over the stark landscape.

SECOND MODEL: Squinting up at the sky, Sara began to kick her foot back and forth in the deep grass.

Betsy Byars, *The Summer of the Swans*

3a.  He was standing there on the court.

3b.  Burt started to dribble the ball up and down.

3c.  He dribbled it on the foul line.

4a.  She was thinking seriously about her friend.

4b.  She began to remember the laughter and tears.

4c.  The laughter and tears were over their many adventures.

# Practice 7: Combining and Imitating

1. Combine each list of sentences to imitate the model.

2. Write your own imitation of the model.

**EXAMPLE** ────────────────────────────────────────────

**Model to Imitate:**

He came up beside me, holding my head in his great clamshell hands.

Theodore Taylor, *The Cay*

**Sentences to Combine:**

a.  She looked out beyond us.

b.  She was searching the horizon.

c.  She was searching it with her large topaz eyes.

**Combination:**

She looked out beyond us, searching the horizon with her large topaz eyes.

**Sample Imitation:**

He came home at noon, bringing the groceries from the new super grocery store.

1. MODEL: Her room stood around her pleasantly, waiting for her.

Louise Fitzhugh, *Harriet the Spy*

a. His dog jumped around him.

b. The dog jumped excitedly.

c. The dog was begging for a treat.

2. MODEL: Remembering the crash, he had a moment of fear, a breath-tightening little rip of terror.

Gary Paulsen, *Hatchet*

a. She was opening the present.

b. She had a smile on her face.

c. The smile was a well-pleased clear expression of delight.

3. MODEL: Smoke, stinking and hideous, leaped like escaping souls from the burning plane wing.

Caroline B. Cooney, *Flight #116 Is Down*

a. Sunshine was dazzling and golden.

b. It shone like yellow watercolors.

c. It shone on the fresh morning horizon.

4. MODEL: Perhaps each of them, listening, glimpsed through that window a private world, unknown to the others.

Elizabeth George Speare, *The Witch of Blackbird Pond*

a. Maybe one of the dogs was straying.

b. While straying, the dog saw in the woods a rabbit.

c. The rabbit was emerging from its warren.

## Activity 1: Sentences

1. Write three sentences about animals.

2. Each sentence should contain a participial phrase to describe the animal.

3. Use each position—opener, s-v split, closer.

**EXAMPLES** ───────────────────────────────────────────

1. Opener: <u>Whinnying in anticipation of being fed its morning breakfast of oats</u>, the pony sauntered toward the fence to greet the twins whose job was to feed it.

2. S-V Split: Two red foxes, <u>racing after each other in a circle like a merry-go-round</u>, surprised the neighborhood early one morning.

3. Closer: At the rim of the pool a dolphin suddenly emerged, <u>wearing a grin on its face</u>.

# Activity 2: Paragraphs

1. Write a paragraph of at least five to eight sentences describing an animal in action: pets or other animals. Choose an animal whose behavior you know well. The examples below are about a lion, penguins, and a fly.

2. Start your paragraph with a topic sentence that shows the animal beginning the action. Then describe in detail the animal's action—a cat stalking a mouse, a dog chasing its tail, a spider spinning a web, a fish exploring its tank, etc.

3. In three or more of the sentences, use a participial phrase to show the actions of the animal.

4. Somewhere in your paragraph, use each position at least once—opener, s-v split, closer.

## EXAMPLES

1. Opener: <u>Treading delicately, like a cat</u>, Aslan the lion stepped from stone to stone across the stream.

   C. S. Lewis, *Prince Caspian*

2. S-V Split: The penguins, <u>now standing politely in two rows of six each</u>, looked curiously at Mr. Greenbaum.

   Richard and Florence Atwater, *Mr. Popper's Penguins*

3. Closer: The fly in the spider web was beating its wings furiously, <u>trying to break loose and free itself</u>.

   E. B. White, *Charlotte's Web*

## Practice 1: Matching

A compound verb is a series of sentence parts that tells two or more actions of a person or thing (the subject of the sentence). A compound verb usually follows the subject and always answers this question:

What series of actions did the subject do?

Two verbs are usually joined by *and*. Three or more verbs are separated with commas alone, or with *and* before the last verb.

### EXAMPLES OF COMPOUND VERBS

Two Verbs: Mr. Wonka <u>spun round</u> and <u>stared at Charlie</u>.

> Roald Dahl, *Charlie and the Chocolate Factory*

Three Verbs: Children <u>crunched potato chips</u>, <u>chomped on pickles</u>, <u>gnawed at fried chicken</u>.

> Beverly Cleary, *Ramona and Her Father*

Four Verbs: The kitten <u>stood up</u>, <u>stretched its small back into a high arch</u>, <u>yawned</u>, and <u>curled up at her feet</u>.

> Madeleine L'Engle, *A Swiftly Tilting Planet*

**Directions:**

1. Match the compound verbs with the sentences.

2. Write out each sentence, inserting and underlining the compound verb.

**Sentences:**

1. Birdie wiped off the girl's tears.

   Lois Lenski, *Strawberry Girl*

2. The milk lady fished two mugs out of a tub of water.

   Sid Fleischman, *The Whipping Boy*

3. A burning limb fell into the pit.

   Jean Craighead George,
   *The Fire Bug Connection*

4. He climbed up a great big tall heaping mountain of snow.

   Ezra Jack Keats, *The Snowy Day*

5. Then I swung my chopping ax high.

   Fred Gipson, *Old Yeller*

6. The spotted twin cats, Romulus and Remus, crawled through the kitchen window.

   Esther Averill, *Jenny and the Cat Club*

**Compound Verbs:**

a. and returned with a large paper package of fish

b. and wheeled, aiming to cave in the bear's head with the first lick

c. and slid all the way down

d. took her to the back porch, and washed her face in the washbasin

e. sat on a stool, and began to milk the cow directly into the mugs

f. struck the water, hissed like a snake, and went out

## Practice 2: Identifying

1.  Review what you learned about compound verbs in Practice 1. Jot down brief answers to these questions on a piece of your paper.

    a.  What information do compound verbs tell?

    b.  Are compound verbs sentences, or sentence parts?

    c.  How long are compound verbs—short, medium, long?

    e.  Where do compound verbs occur in a sentence?

    f.  When are commas used for compound verbs?

    g.  How can compound verbs improve your writing?

2.  Find the compound verbs in these sentences, and see if your answers fit them.

1. Ramona scowled and slid down in her chair.

   Beverly Cleary, *Ramona and Her Father*

2. They took him away and shut him in a prison.

   Hans Augusto Rey, *Curious George*

3. The large woman simply turned around and kicked him right square in his blue-jeaned sitter.

   Langston Hughes, "Thank You, M'am"

4. They climbed narrow steps and opened creaking doors to three small rooms with beds under dust covers.

   Donna Hill, "Ghost Cat"

5. I let out a terrified howl, scrambled to my feet, and lurched away from his bony, outstretched hand.

   R. L. Stine, *Ghost Beach*

6. He nose-dived into the grass, turned a somersault, rolled over a few times on the steep slope, and landed on the next ant heap, six feet away.

   Dick King-Smith, *Pigs Might Fly*

© 2000 by Don and Jenny Killgallon from *Sentence Composing for Elementary School*. Portsmouth, NH: Heinemann.

# Practice 3: Combining

1. Combine the two sentences by making the <u>underlined parts</u> of the second sentence a compound verb to put at the caret (^).

2. Write the new sentence and underline the compound verbs.

## EXAMPLE

**Sentences to Combine:**

a. The shark paused ^.

b. <u>And</u> the shark <u>stared up at the company with small evil eyes</u>.

**Combination:**

The shark <u>paused</u> and <u>stared up at the company with small evil eyes</u>.

Roald Dahl, *James and the Giant Peach*

1a. With these words, the Witch fell down in a melted shapeless mass ^.

1b. <u>And</u> she <u>began to spread over the kitchen floor</u>.

> L. Frank Baum, *The Wizard of Oz*

2a. Very quietly, the two girls groped their way among the other sleepers ^.

2b. <u>And</u> the two girls <u>crept out of the tent</u>.

> C. S. Lewis, *The Lion, the Witch, and the Wardrobe*

3a. Garlands of flowers hung from every house and shop ^.

3b. <u>And</u> they <u>carpeted the streets</u>.

> Norton Juster, *The Phantom Tollbooth*

4a. Sara curled herself up in the window-seat, ^.

4b. She <u>opened a book, and began to read</u>.

> Frances Hodgson Burnett, *A Little Princess*

5a. Then Beezus came into the kitchen through the back door, ^.

5b. Beezus <u>dropped her books on the table, and flopped down on a chair with a gusty sigh</u>.

> Beverly Cleary, *Ramona and Her Father*

6a. The king gripped the arms of the chair, ^.

6b. He <u>closed his eyes, clenched his teeth, and sweated</u>.

> T. H. White, *Book of Merlyn*

# Practice 4: Unscrambling

1. Unscramble the list of sentence parts and write out the sentence.

2. Underline the sentence parts that are compound verbs. NOTE: The capitalized sentence part begins the sentence.

---

**EXAMPLE**

**Scrambled Sentence Parts:**

a. and began climbing toward the heavens

b. The giant peach rose up

c. dripping out of the water

**Unscrambled Sentence:**

The giant peach <u>rose up dripping out of the water</u> and <u>began climbing toward the heavens</u>.

Roald Dahl, James and the Giant Peach

© 2000 by Don and Jenny Killgallon from Sentence Composing for Elementary School. Portsmouth, NH: Heinemann.

1a. The Monkeys flew the Tinman

1b. and dropped him on sharp rocks

1c. high in the air

L. Frank Baum, *The Wizard of Oz*

2a. and began

2b. Leslie whirled

2c. to duel the imaginary foe

Katherine Paterson, *Bridge to Terabithia*

3a. then smiled

3b. She took a deep breath

3c. and patted the rabbit on its head

Lois Lenski, *Strawberry Girl*

4a. and broke it

4b. She grabbed the little gold chain

4c. yanked with all her strength

Lois Lowry, *Number the Stars*

5a. and went downstairs

5b. pushed her feet into furry slippers

5c. She got out of bed

Madeleine L'Engle, *A Swiftly Tilting Planet*

6a. and, on wintry nights, lay at the Judge's feet before the roaring fire

6b. carried the Judge's grandsons on his back

6c. The dog escorted the Judge's daughters on rambles

Jack London, *The Call of the Wild*

## Practice 5: Expanding

1. Create compound verbs that begin with the words provided.

2. Vary the lengths of the compound verbs—some short, some medium, some long.

**EXAMPLE** ————————————————————————————————

**Sentence:**

She switched on the light and left . . . .

**Sample Compound Verbs:**

Short:      left quickly

Medium:   left on her way upstairs

Long:       left before anyone spoke to her about the argument over the championship game

**Original Sentence:**

She switched on the light and left the door open.

Langston Hughes, "Thank You, M'am"

1. He fell with his leg twisted under him and could hear. . . .

   Lois Lowry, *The Giver*

2. He tumbled upside down and reached. . . .

   Sam McBratney, *Guess How Much I Love You*

3. Suddenly, a slim white cat sped through the grass, dashed . . . , and began. . . .

   Esther Averill, *Jenny and the Cat Club*

4. Now and again strangers came, gave . . . , and took. . . .

   Jack London, *The Call of the Wild*

5. Bradley scribbled, cut . . . , and taped. . . .

   Louis Sachar, *There's a Boy in the Girls' Bathroom*

6. At that moment, Patsy raced in, threw . . . , snatched . . . , and made. . . .

   Paula Fox, *Maurice's Room*

7. Mrs. Jones stopped, jerked . . . , put . . . , and continued. . . .

   Langston Hughes, "Thank You, M'am"

8. The Giant crept . . . and opened . . . and went. . . .

   Oscar Wilde, "The Selfish Giant"

9. The boy put the dog's dish under the porch, closed . . . , pushed . . . , sat . . . , and began. . . .

   William H. Armstrong, *Sounder*

10. He cut poles and slung . . . , quickly laid . . . , gathered . . . , and built. . . .

    Hal Borland, *When the Legends Die*

# Practice 6: Unscrambling to Imitate

1. Unscramble both lists of sentence parts to imitate the same model.

2. Imitate the arrangement of sentence parts in the model.

**EXAMPLE** ———————————————————————

**Model to Imitate:**

Then she reached down, picked the boy up by his shirt front, and shook him until his teeth rattled.

Langston Hughes, "Thank You, M'am"

**Lists:**

a. and opened the escape hatch as the plane descended

b. pulled the lever down by its red handle

c. quickly Cranston looked up


a. and hit the ground as the rest followed

b. jumped the fence smoothly in a quick movement

c. suddenly the deer gazed around

**Imitations:**

Quickly Cranston looked up, pulled the lever down by its red handle, and opened the escape hatch as the plane descended.


Suddenly the deer gazed around, jumped the fence smoothly in a quick movement, and hit the ground as the rest followed.

FIRST MODEL: I sat down, picked up my spoon, and splashed it down into my oatmeal.

Rosa Guy, *The Friends*

1a. got out his license

1b. on the dashboard

1c. He pulled over

1d. and put it out


2a. and wrote it all down

2b. She listened carefully

2c. on one page

2d. took out her notebook

SECOND MODEL: Jonas unstrapped Gabe, lifted him from the bike, and watched him investigate the grass and twigs with delight.

Lois Lowry, *The Giver*

3a. and heard it slap

3b. Frank anchored the boat

3c. the water and seagrass in rhythm

3d. moved it out of the sun


4a. moved her toward the barn

4b. navigate the barnyard and stall doors with impatience

4c. and saw the cow

4d. Susan fed Buttercup

# Practice 7: Unscrambling and Imitating

1. Unscramble the list of sentence parts to imitate the model.

2. Write your own imitation of the model.

**EXAMPLE** ────────────────────────────────

**Model to Imitate:**

Jonas reached the other side of the river, stopped briefly, and looked back.

Lois Lowry, *The Giver*

**Scrambled Sentence Parts:**

a. moved slowly

b. He picked up the heavy lid of the container

c. and set it down

**Unscrambled Sentence:**

He picked up the heavy lid of the container, moved slowly, and set it down.

**Sample Imitation:**

The driver hit the air brakes of the truck, breathed sharply, and leaned forward.

# Using Compound Verbs

1. MODEL: Harry rummaged once more in his trunk, extracted his money bag, and shoved some gold into Stan's hand.

J. K. Rowling, *Harry Potter and the Prisoner of Azkaban*

   a. and questioned the class about the correct location

   b. the teacher went once again to the board

   c. drew the map

2. MODEL: The creatures swung upward, hung poised against the sky for an instant, then climbed swiftly, and sped westward.

Lloyd Alexander, *The Book of Three*

   a. then flew unexpectedly

   b. the ladybug crawled out

   c. stood quietly inside the grass of the lawn

   d. and disappeared quickly

3. MODEL: Justin was out with a mighty leap, hit the floor with a thump, and ran, disappearing from my view, heading toward the end of the room.

Robert C. O'Brien, *Mrs. Frisby and the Rats of NIMH*

   a. and glowed, filling the sky with warmth

   b. the sun came up with a burst of color

   c. spilling across the fields of clover

   d. covered the horizon with light

4. MODEL: The rooster ruffled his wings, hopped over to stand beside the pig, filled his throat with air, and foolishly crowed.

Bill and Vera Cleaver, *Where the Lilies Bloom*

   a. raised his voice with authority

   b. the referee blew his whistle

   c. and quickly negotiated

   d. bent down to retrieve the ball

# Activity 1: Sentences

1. Write three sentences showing people in a series of actions described in the compound verbs.

2. In one sentence, use two verbs; in another sentence, use three verbs; and in another sentence, use four verbs.

3. Study the authors' sentences below to try to make your sentences as good as theirs.

**EXAMPLES** ───────────────────────────────────────

1. <u>Two Verbs</u>: He caught the fish with his bare hands and ate them with his rice.

    Steven J. Myers, "The Enchanted Sticks"

2. <u>Three Verbs</u>: Arnold pressed down the bottom wire, thrust a leg through, and leaned forward to bring the other leg after.

    Gina Berriault, "The Stone Boy"

3. <u>Four Verbs</u>: Gwydion struck out after him, soon overtook him, seized him by the hair, and drew him toward the shallows.

    Lloyd Alexander, *The Book of Three*

## Activity 2: Paragraphs

1. Write a paragraph of five to eight sentences showing an athlete in action: football player, ice skater, gymnast, pitcher, goalie, diver, swimmer, jogger, weight lifter, etc.

2. Start your paragraph with a topic sentence that shows the athlete beginning the action. Then describe in detail the athlete continuing the action—the race, the pitch, the skating competition, the dive, etc.

3. Include many compound verbs describing one part of the race, pitch, skating competition, dive, etc. Study the underlined examples below.

**EXAMPLE: A FOOTBALL PLAYER** ————————————————————————

(1) The pass was high and wide and Darling jumped for it. (2) Darling picked his feet up high and delicately ran over a blocker and an opposing linesman in a jumble on the ground near the scrimmage line. (3) He had ten yards in the clear and picked up speed. (4) The first halfback came at him, and he fed him his leg, then swung at the last moment, took the shock of the man's shoulder without breaking stride, and ran through him. (6) There was only the safety man now. (7) Darling tucked the ball in and spurted at him. (8) He was sure he was going to get past the safety man. (9) Without thought, he headed right for the safety man and stiff-armed him, feeling blood spurt instantaneously from the man's nose onto his hand. (10) He pivoted away, dropping the safety man as he ran easily toward the goal line.

Irwin Shaw, "The Eighty-Yard Run" (adapted)

## Practice 1: Matching

An adjective clause is a sentence part that makes a statement about a person, place, or thing named in a sentence. Adjective clauses usually begin with one of these words: *who, which, whose*. Because they are clauses, they contain a subject and verb. They answer these questions, and begin with the words in parentheses:

What did the person, place, or thing do? (*who, which*)

What did the person, place, or thing have? (*whose*)

Adjective clauses occur between a subject and verb (*subject-verb split*), or at the end of a sentence (*closer*).

### EXAMPLES OF ADJECTIVE CLAUSES ———————————————————

*Who:* The twins, <u>who had finished their homework</u>, were allowed to watch half an hour of TV. (subject-verb split)

> Madeleine L'Engle, *A Wrinkle in Time*

*Which:* The man on the loudspeaker begins calling everyone over to the track for the first event, <u>which is the 20-yard dash</u>. (closer)

> Toni Cade Bambara, *Raymond's Run*

*Whose:* Little Jon, <u>whose eyes were quicker than most</u>, should have seen the hole, but all his attention was on the stars. (subject-verb split)

> Alexander Key, *The Forgotten Door*

### Directions:

1. Match the adjective clauses with the sentences.

2. Write out each sentence, inserting and underlining the adjective clause.

3. Use both positions at least once—subject-verb split, closer.

**Sentences:**

1. Gwydion caught sight of them instantly.

   Lloyd Alexander, *The Book of Three*

2. Sara opened the paper bag and took out one of the hot buns.

   Frances Hodgson Burnett,
   *A Little Princess*

3. Ramo was standing on one foot and then the other, watching the ship coming.

   Scott O'Dell, *Island of the Blue Dolphins*

4. The old woman was beside him hunched over as she shuffled along in her soft slippers.

   Lois Lowry, *The Giver*

5. Heidi stopped to admire her.

   Johanna Spyri, *Heidi*

6. The little prince never seemed to hear the ones I asked him.

   Antoine De Saint-Exupéry,
   *The Little Prince*

**Adjective Clauses:**

a. who had never seen so huge a cat

b. who asked me so many questions

c. which had already warmed her own cold hands a little

d. which he did not know was a ship because he had never seen one

e. whose eyes were everywhere at once

f. whose arm he held

## Practice 2: Identifying

1. Review what you learned about adjective clauses in Practice 1. Jot down brief answers to these questions on a piece of your paper.

  a. What information do adjective clauses tell?

  b. Are adjective clauses sentences, or sentence parts?

  c. What words usually begin adjective clauses?

  d. How long are adjective clauses—short, medium, long?

  e. Where can adjective clauses be placed in a sentence?

  f. When is one comma used for an adjective clause? Two commas?

  g. How can adjective clauses improve your writing?

2. Find the adjective clauses in these sentences, and see if your answers fit them.

1. Susie was a sleek, excited matron of some three hundred pounds, who reared herself out of the water as they approached.

   Arthur C. Clarke, *Dolphin Island*

2. Little Jon, whose eyes were quicker than most, should have seen the hole, but all his attention was on the stars.

   Alexander Key, *The Forgotten Door*

3. There was a gate in the wall, whose locks were jawbones set with sharp teeth.

   Post Wheeler, "Vasilissa the Beautiful"

4. It was a dog, which hopped along on three legs, crying softly and holding up a front paw.

   Gertrude Chandler Warner, *The Boxcar Children*

5. Sandy and Dennis, her ten-year-old twin brothers, who got home from school an hour earlier than she did, were disgusted.

   Madeleine L'Engle, *A Wrinkle in Time*

6. Miss Crocker walked stiffly to her desk, which was set on a tiny platform and piled high with bulky objects covered by a tarpaulin.

   Mildred D. Taylor, *Roll of Thunder, Hear My Cry*

# Practice 3: Combining

1. Combine the two sentences by making the <u>underlined part</u> of the second sentence an adjective clause to put at the caret (^).

2. Write the new sentence and underline the adjective clause.

**EXAMPLE** ——————————————————————————————

**Sentences to Combine:**

a. Even Mrs. Callahan, ^, made a lovely frozen custard for him.

b. She was someone <u>who had never had a very high opinion of Captain Cook</u>.

**Combination:**

Even Mrs. Callahan, <u>who had never had a very high opinion of Captain Cook</u>, made a lovely frozen custard for him.

> Richard and Florence Atwater, *Mr. Popper's Penguins*

1a. The great coon dog, ^, came from under the porch and began to whine.

1b. It was the dog <u>whose rhythmic panting came through the porch floor</u>.

William H. Armstrong, *Sounder*

2a. Benny caught the boy by the shoulder before he could run to the bear, ^.

2b. It was the bear <u>which was bawling and snapping at the chair</u>.

Hal Borland, *When the Legends Die*

3a. Boysie, ^, heard the door shut and came to the living room.

3b. It was Boysie <u>who slept in the kitchen</u>.

Betsy Byars, *The Summer of the Swans*

4a. The stallion neighed encouragement to his mares, ^, fighting the wreckage and the sea.

4b. They were the mares <u>who were struggling to keep afloat</u>.

Marguerite Henry, *Misty of Chincoteague*

5a. The old woman's voice was fading, and she named the gift very softly, but her daughter, ^, was weeping and did not hear.

5b. It was the daughter <u>who loved her greatly</u>.

Lois Duncan, *A Gift of Magic*

6a. Behind her in the shadows, he could see the little boy, ^.

6b. It was the boy <u>who must have been about his own age</u>.

Madeleine L'Engle, *A Wrinkle in Time*

# Practice 4: Unscrambling

1. Unscramble the list of sentence parts and write out the sentence.

2. Underline the sentence parts that are adjective clauses. NOTE: The capitalized sentence part begins the sentence.

---

**EXAMPLE** ─────────────────────────────────────────

**Scrambled Sentence Parts:**

a. who was close to tears by now

b. told the truth

c. Mrs. Posey

**Unscrambled Sentence:**

Mrs. Posey, <u>who was close to tears by now</u>, told the truth.

Jean Merrill, The Pushcart War

1a. into her hands

1b. He put the big blood heart

1c. which was still beating

> Willard Price, "The Killer Shark"

2a. turned now to stare at him

2b. The sheep

2c. who had moved slightly away as he had come into the pasture

> Katherine Paterson, *Park's Quest*

3a. with two of his fingers missing

3b. There was Crook Arm

3c. whose left arm dangled down uselessly by his side

> Laurence Yep, *Dragonwings*

4a. so that she might not see the love in his eyes

4b. On her way back she met the Prince

4c. who pulled up his horse and scowled at her

> Elinor Mordaunt, "The Prince and the Goose Girl"

5a. which she got down the boy's throat with no little difficulty

5b. One piece of aspirin flew out of sight under the stove, and the other piece

5c. came up again promptly along with the bowl of soup she had coaxed down

> Katherine Paterson, *The Great Gilly Hopkins*

6a. who was pushing a book back upon the desk

6b. Miss Crocker was sitting at Miss Davis's desk

6c. staring fiercely down at Little Man

> Mildred D. Taylor, *Roll of Thunder, Hear My Cry*

# Practice 5: Expanding

1.  Create an adjective clause that begins with the words provided.

2.  Vary the lengths of the adjective clauses—some short, some medium, some long.

**EXAMPLE** ———————————————————————————————

**Sentence:**

All the eyes of Paris were fixed on the Eiffel Tower, which. . . .

**Sample Adjective Clauses:**

Short:      which everyone knew

Medium:   which was the famous tourist attraction

Long:       which was the place most loved by the city's population

**Original Sentence:**

All the eyes of Paris were fixed on the Eiffel Tower, <u>which slowly drooped over as if it were made of soft rubber</u>.

Chris Van Allsburg, The Sweetest Fig

1. Harry was a white dog with black spots, who. . . .

    Gene Zion, *Harry the Dirty Dog*

2. She also had to watch our three chickens, who. . . .

    Laurence Yep, *Dragonwings*

3. Stacey, who . . . , shook his head.

    Mildred D. Taylor, *Roll of Thunder, Hear My Cry*

4. When she couldn't stand it anymore, she kicked off the blankets and walked over to her Barbie doll, which. . . .

    Gary Soto, "Barbie"

5. Across the stalk land into the pine woods, into the climbing, brightening glow of dawn, the boy followed the dog, whose. . . .

    William H. Armstrong, *Sounder*

6. Gwydion, who . . . , **rose and spoke to the companions.**

    Lloyd Alexander, *The High King*

7. Nurse, who . . . , watched approvingly while he ate a hearty meal of eggs, canned meat, and tropical fruit.

    Arthur C. Clarke, *Dolphin Island*

8. Her dear mamma, who . . . , had been French.

    Frances Hodgson Burnett, *A Little Princess*

9. That night he kept a fire going and sat watching for the lion, which. . . .

    Hal Borland, *When the Legends Die*

10. This leader, whose . . . , was no more than twelve or thirteen years old and looked even younger.

    Henry Gregor Felsen, "Horatio"

# Practice 6: Combining to Imitate

1. Combine both lists of sentences to imitate the same model.

2. Change the first sentence into the first sentence part of the model, and change the second sentence into the second sentence part of the model, etc.

---

**EXAMPLE**

**Model to Imitate:**

Miss Minchin came into the room, accompanied by a sharp-featured, dry little gentleman, who looked rather disturbed.

Frances Hodgson Burnett, *A Little Princess*

**Lists:**

a. The parents walked along the beach.

b. They were accompanied by their cutely-dressed, adorable child.

c. It was a child who seemed very excited.

a. The droid raced toward the spacecraft.

b. It was powered by a battery-operated embedded microprocessor.

c. It was a microprocessor which worked extremely well.

**Imitations:**

The parents walked along the beach, accompanied by their cutely-dressed, adorable child, who seemed very excited.

The droid raced toward the spacecraft, powered by a battery-operated, embedded microprocessor, which worked extremely well.

FIRST MODEL: Romey and Ima Dean and Devola, who had banished themselves during the visit, came around the corner of the house.

Bill and Vera Cleaver, *Where the Lilies Bloom*

1a. It was Roland and Freddie and Chamon.

1b. They were the ones who had talked themselves out of trouble.

1c. They stood quietly at the back of the room.


2a. It was Mattie and Sarah and Eve.

2b. They were the ones who had reassured themselves during the storm.

2c. They walked outside the shed near the barn.


SECOND MODEL: Above the smoke-blackened fortress and the burial mound, whose fresh earth was already frost-covered, the clouds had grown heavy.

Lloyd Alexander, *The High King*

3a. It was under the back porch and the old steps.

3b. These were the steps whose planks were always rotting.

3c. The treasure had remained undiscovered.


4a. It was near the oak tree and the barn.

4b. It was the barn whose doors were wide open.

4c. The puppies had found safety.


© 2000 by Don and Jenny Killgallon from *Sentence Composing for Elementary School*. Portsmouth, NH: Heinemann.

# Practice 7: Combining and Imitating

1. Combine each list of sentences to imitate the model.

2. Write your own imitation of the model.

**EXAMPLE** ────────────────────────────────

**Model to Imitate:**

By afternoon, Perrault, who was in a hurry to be on the trail to Dawson with his dispatches, returned with three more dogs.

Jack London, The Call of the Wild

**Sentences to Combine:**

a. It happened by morning.

b. Tony brought them a good meal.

c. Tony was the one who was hoping to feed the children with breakfast.

**Combination:**

By morning, Tony, who was hoping to feed the children with breakfast, brought them a good meal.

**Sample Imitation:**

By midnight, Terence, who was in a mood to be reckoned with by the others, issued several important commands.

1. MODEL: Even his eyes, which had been young, looked old.

   John Steinbeck, *The Red Pony*

   a. It was also the pen.

   b. It was the one which had been new.

   c. It seemed broken.

2. MODEL: Little Nutbrown Hare, who was going to bed, held on tight to Big Nutbrown Hare's very long ears.

   Sam McBratney, *Guess How Much I Love You*

   a. It was Meg.

   b. She was the one who was reading the book.

   c. She looked very closely at the utterly beautiful illustrations.

3. MODEL: Slowly I peeled off my black sweater, which I wear practically all the time, and stuffed it in my bottom drawer under my bathing suit.

   Emily Neville, *It's Like This, Cat*

   a. Slowly I copied down the popular lyric.

   b. It was the one which I listen to every day.

   c. And I put it in my notebook behind the math problems.

4. MODEL: He pictured his father, who must have been a shy and quiet boy, for he was a shy and quiet man, seated within his group, waiting to be called to the stage.

   Lois Lowry, *The Giver*

   a. He thought about his friend.

   b. He was the one who must have been a happy and healthy baby, for he was a happy and healthy boy.

   c. His friend was excited after his speech, hoping to be chosen by their classmates.

# Activity 1: Sentences

1. Write two sentences about people and two sentences about animals.

2. Each sentence should contain an adjective clause to describe the person (beginning with *who*) or the animal (beginning with *which*).

3. Use each position—subject-verb split, closer.

## EXAMPLES

1. PERSON (subject-verb split): Miss Fleetie Breathitt, <u>who was the principal of our school as well as my teacher and sometimes Romey's</u>, said she was glad to see us again.

   Bill and Vera Cleaver, *Where the Lilies Bloom*

2. PERSON (closer): Behind her in the shadows, he could see the little boy, <u>who must have been about his own age</u>.

   Madeleine L'Engle, *A Wrinkle in Time*

3. ANIMAL (subject-verb split): The pig, <u>which was a young one</u>, made oinking noises and Kiser, chewing on his toothpick, said I was wasting my time trying to scare him off with looks.

   Bill and Vera Cleaver, *Where the Lilies Bloom*

4. ANIMAL (closer): That night he kept a fire going and sat watching for the lion, <u>which came and prowled the nearby darkness</u>.

   Hal Borland, *When the Legends Die*

# Activity 2: Paragraphs

1. Add detail to the paragraph below by writing an adjective clause to describe any *four* underlined items.

2. Use each of these words at least once: *who, which, whose.*

**PARAGRAPH TO EXPAND** ─────────────────────────────────

(1) Taking tickets at the <u>cineplex</u>, the <u>usher</u> greeted everyone with a smile. (2) A high school student employed by the movie theater for the summer, she always was neatly dressed in a <u>uniform</u>. (3) Noticing a family with several little children approaching, she imagined that they were going to see <u>the biggest blockbuster of the summer</u>. (4) When the <u>parents</u> handed her the tickets to a different movie, she was delighted to see <u>the movie they had chosen</u>. (5) <u>She and the rest of the theater's employees</u> had seen and loved the movie at a special preview.

# Practice 1: Matching

An adverb clause is a sentence part that gives details about the main event in a sentence. Because they are clauses, they contain a subject and verb. They answer these questions, and begin with the words in parentheses:

When did it happen? (*as, when, while, before, after, until*)

Why did it happen? (*because, since*)

Under what conditions? (*if, although*)

Adverb clauses occur at the beginning of a sentence (*opener*), between a subject and verb (*subject-verb split*), or at the end of a sentence (*closer*). One comma is used for an opener, two for a subject-verb split, and usually none for a closer.

## EXAMPLES OF ADVERB CLAUSES ──────────────────────

Opener: <u>While she sat there</u>, a fuzzy spider paced across the room.

> Eleanor Coerr, *Sadako and the Thousand Paper Cranes*

S-V Split: Mrs. Rachel, <u>before she had closed the door</u>, had taken mental note of everything that was on that table.

> L. M. Montgomery, *Anne of Green Gables*

Closer: Her voice softened <u>as she looked at the sleepy little boy</u>.

> Mildred D. Taylor, *Song of the Trees*

## Directions:

1. Match the adverb clauses with the sentences.

2. Write out each sentence, inserting and underlining the adverb clause.

3. Use all three positions at least once—opener, subject-verb split, closer.

## Sentences:

1. The children in the school across the street couldn't keep their eyes on their lessons.

   > Virginia Lee Burton,
   > *Mike Mulligan and His Steam Shovel*

2. I decided to tell it that way.

   > Jean Fritz, *Homesick: My Own Story*

3. Each night, Mother Bat would carry Stellaluna clutched to her breast.

   > Janell Cannon, *Stellaluna*

4. The first floor was where the rats lived.

   > Walter Dean Myers,
   > *Motown and Didi: A Love Story*

5. His voice seemed sad.

   > Theodore Taylor, *The Cay*

6. At least he had no place to go which required good clothes.

   > John Steinbeck, *The Red Pony*

## Adverb Clauses:

a. although he was trying to be cheerful

b. because it was closest to the garbage in the empty lot

c. when they heard the fire engine

d. if he had no good clothes

e. since my childhood feels like a story

f. as she flew out to search for food

# Practice 2: Identifying

1.  Review what you learned about adverb clauses in Practice 1. Jot down brief answers to these questions on a piece of your paper.

   a.  What information do adverb clauses tell?

   b.  Are adverb clauses sentences, or sentence parts?

   c.  What words usually begin adverb clauses?

   d.  How long are adverb clauses—short, medium, long?

   e.  Where can adverb clauses be placed in a sentence?

   f.  When is one comma used for an adverb clause? Two commas? Usually none?

   g.  How can adverb clauses improve your writing?

2.  Find the adverb clauses in these sentences, and see if your answers fit them.

1. They crossed one deep valley, then another, before Gurgi halted on a ridge.

    Lloyd Alexander, *The Book of Three*

2. When flour was scarce, the boy's mother would wrap the leftover biscuits in a clean flour sack and put them away for the next meal.

    William H. Armstrong, *Sounder*

3. The penguin chicks, when they began to hatch, were not so handsomely marked as their mother and father.

    Florence and Richard Atwater, *Mr. Popper's Penguins*

4. When the tinkling little melody began, Winnie's sobbing slowed.

    Natalie Babbitt, *Tuck Everlasting*

5. As she let herself in through the gleaming white front door, her father appeared in the double doors of the living room.

    Lynne Reid Banks, *One More River*

6. Her face, when he stepped into the light, was round and thick, and her eyes were like two immense eggs stuck into a white mess of bread dough.

    Ray Bradbury, *The Martian Chronicles*

## Practice 3: Combining

1. Combine the two sentences by making the <u>underlined part</u> of the second sentence an adverb clause to put at the caret (^) .

2. Write the new sentence and underline the adverb clause.

**EXAMPLE** ———————————————————————————

**Sentences to Combine:**

a. She dropped her books on the sidewalk ^.

b. She did this <u>while she gave a good scratch</u>.

**Combination:**

She dropped her books on the sidewalk <u>while she gave a good scratch</u>.

Toni Cade Bambara, "Geraldine Moore the Poet"

1a. He began to dig again, driving the spade deep into the rich, black garden soil ^.

1b. He did this <u>while the robin hopped about very busily employed</u>.

Frances Hodgson Burnett, *The Secret Garden*

2a. ^ She found she could not open the door.

2b. This happened <u>when Miss Munchkin sent her sister, Miss Amelia, to see what the child was doing</u>.

Frances Hodgson Burnett, *A Little Princess*

3a. The second box, ^, was filled with papers.

3b. She saw this <u>as she moved on to it</u>.

Lois Duncan, *A Gift of Magic*

4a. ^ I took him in my arms and set out walking once more.

4b. I did this <u>as the little prince dropped off to sleep</u>.

Antoine De Saint-Exupéry, *The Little Prince*

5a. She would not need a calender or a clock ^,

5b. She would not need them <u>if she knew enough about nature</u>.

Jean Craighead George, *The Fire Bug Connection*

6a. ^ I packed my suitcase and told my mother I was going to run away.

6b. I did this <u>when I was in elementary school</u>.

Jean Craighead George, *My Side of the Mountain*

## Practice 4: Unscrambling

1. Unscramble the list of sentence parts and write out the sentence.

2. Underline the sentence parts that are adverb clauses. NOTE: The capitalized sentence part begins the sentence.

**EXAMPLE** ───────────────────────────────────

**Scrambled Sentence Parts:**

a. at Mrs. Callahan's striped stockings

b. Popper pulled obediently at the clothesline

c. while Captain Cook took a parting peck

**Unscrambled Sentence:**

Popper pulled obediently at the clothesline <u>while Captain Cook took a parting peck at Mrs. Callahan's stockings</u>.

Richard and Florence Atwater, *Mr. Popper's Penguins*

1a.  and hauled him to Melyngar's back

1b.  While Taran struggled to his feet

1c.  Gwydion seized him like a sack of meal

Lloyd Alexander, *The Book of Three*


2a.  stuck in her hair

2b.  The bright autumn leaves

2c.  as she twisted her head back and forth

Lynne Reid Banks, *One More River*


3a.  shut tight

3b.  Although he could tell it was daylight

3c.  he kept his eyes

J. K. Rowling, *Harry Potter and the Sorcerer's Stone*


4a.  as she watched a dried leaf scratch along the driveway in the autumn wind

4b.  around her knees

4c.  She wrapped her arms

Beverly Cleary, *Ramona and Her Father*


5a.  to fold only one paper crane

5b.  Before she went to sleep

5c.  Sadako managed

Eleanor Coerr, *Sadako and the Thousand Paper Cranes*


6a.  and carried the silvery ball to her hideout

6b.  While Maggie watched

6c.  the spider rolled up her web

Jean Craighead George, *The Fire Bug Connection*

# Practice 5: Expanding

1. Create an adverb clause that begins with the words provided.

2. Vary the lengths of the adverb clauses—some short, some medium, some long.

**EXAMPLE** ——————————————————————————————

**Sentence:**

One night Jonas fell when . . .

**Sample Adverb Clauses:**

Short:     when he tripped

Medium:   when he looked up from the path

Long:      when the lights of an oncoming car caught him at just the wrong angle

**Original Sentence:**

One night Jonas fell <u>when the bike jolted to a sudden stop against a rock</u>.

Lois Lowry, *The Giver*

1. When . . . , I felt as if everybody must be looking at me and pitying me.

   L. M. Montgomery, *Anne of Green Gables*

2. The truck drivers, when . . . , were furious.

   Jean Merrill, *The Pushcart War*

3. The superintendent, Fred Snood, checked the cellar storage cages, after. . . .

   Emily Neville, *It's Like This, Cat*

4. While . . . , I saw the big gray dog, the leader of the wild pack, in the brush above me.

   Scott O'Dell, *Island of the Blue Dolphins*

5. Miss Ellis flinched at the pop of Gilly's gum but continued to talk in her calm, professional voice while. . . .

   Katherine Paterson, *The Great Gilly Hopkins*

6. Although . . . , each day he arrived home looking as if his pants had not been washed in more than a month.

   Mildred D. Taylor, *Roll of Thunder, Hear My Cry*

7. If . . . , Bibot was sure to teach him a lesson.

   Chris Van Allsburg, *The Sweetest Fig*

8. While . . . , Anna's father went around to the back door of the van to take down her wheelchair.

   Larry Weinberg, *Ghost Hotel*

9. Dicey was up and dressed, washed and fed, and out the door, with the day's work outlined in her head, before. . . .

   Cynthia Voigt, *Seventeen Against the Dealer*

10. When . . . , it's hard to sleep.

    E. B. White, *Charlotte's Web*

# Practice 6: Unscrambling to Imitate

1. Unscramble both lists of sentence parts to imitate the same model.

2. Imitate the arrangement of sentence parts in the model.

## EXAMPLE

**Model to Imitate:**

When Papa saw us, he began running swiftly, easily, like the wind.

Mildred D. Taylor, *Roll of Thunder, Hear My Cry*

**Lists:**

a. like a jack-hammer

b. the carpenter started hammering loudly, constantly

c. while his boss gave instructions

a. like a Cheshire cat

b. Ally was smiling easily, broadly

c. as the coach praised her

**Imitations:**

While his boss gave instructions, the carpenter started hammering loudly, constantly, like a jack-hammer.

As the coach praised her, Ally was smiling easily, broadly, like a Cheshire cat.

# Using Adverb Clauses

FIRST MODEL: When Mr. Zuckerman reached the pigpen, he climbed over the fence and poured the slops into the trough.

E. B. White, *Charlotte's Web*

1a.  with his siblings

1b.  and shared his new book

1c.  after Brennan opened the package

1d.  he ran into the family room


2a.  on her napkin

2b.  when Kylie ate the cookie

2c.  and made a pile

2d.  she removed the yucky raisins

SECOND MODEL: On Sunday afternoons, if the weather was good, crowds of people would gather on the shores of Bird Lake, and Louis would give a concert.

E. B. White, *The Trumpet of the Swan*

3a.  when the sun was shining

3b.  and employees would sell them mulch

3c.  in early spring

3d.  all the gardeners would go to the stores in their neighborhoods


4a.  and Prentice would imitate their father's behavior

4b.  if their parents were asleep

4c.  all of the children would sit on the floor of the den

4d.  on Saturday mornings

# Practice 7: Unscrambling and Imitating

1. Unscramble the list of sentence parts to imitate the model.

2. Write your own imitation of the model.

**EXAMPLE** ───────────────────────────────────

**Model to Imitate:**

If eyes hadn't been shining out of the deep, dark sockets, the man in the shadows might have been a corpse.

J. K. Rowling, *Harry Potter and the Prisoner of Azkaban*

**Scrambled Sentence Parts:**

a. couldn't have fixed the garbage disposal

b. if electricity hadn't been turned off at the circuit breaker

c. the plumber under the sink

**Unscrambled Sentence:**

If electricity hadn't been turned off at the circuit breaker, the plumber under the sink couldn't have fixed the garbage disposal.

**Sample Imitation:**

If the dogs hadn't been running wild in the first place, the garbage in the backyard would have stayed in the trash cans.

1. MODEL: When a Trumpeter Swan hits an enemy with its wing, it is like being hit by a baseball bat.

   E. B. White, *The Trumpet of the Swan*

   a. it is like

   b. when a small child cries bitter tears over a lost toy

   c. watching rains from a sudden storm

2. MODEL: When Harry the Dirty Dog got to his house, he crawled through the fence and sat looking at the back door.

   Gene Zion, *Harry the Dirty Dog*

   a. he waited on the counter

   b. and began thinking about the other vegetables

   c. when Lou the New Carrot got chosen for the salad

3. MODEL: As nails gave way and boards of the box splintered, I heard several puppy whimpers.

   Wilson Rawls, *Where the Red Fern Grows*

   a. and books of the students appeared

   b. as chairs pushed back

   c. she saw many smiling faces

4. MODEL: As he was crossing Strawberry Hill, thinking of some of the many, many things he could wish for, he was startled to see a mean, hungry lion looking right at him from behind some tall grass.

   William Steig, *Sylvester and the Magic Pebble*

   a. she was delighted to watch an excited, enthusiastic group

   b. as she was passing the museum

   c. going up the steps toward the large entrance

   d. thinking about the many, many exhibits she had helped create

# Activity 1: Sentences

1. Write three sentences about people.

2. Each sentence should contain an adverb clause to describe a person.

3. Use each position—opener, subject-verb split, closer

**EXAMPLES**

1. Opener: <u>After Billy left him and walked angrily away</u>, Jody turned up toward the house.

   John Steinbeck, *The Red Pony*

2. S-V Split: Her face, <u>when he stepped into the light</u>, was round and thick, and her eyes were like two immense eggs stuck into a white mess of bread dough.

   Ray Bradbury, *The Martian Chronicles*

3. Closer: The thunder was creeping closer now, rolling angrily over the forest depths and bringing the lightning with it, <u>as we emerged from the path into the deserted Avery yard</u>.

   Mildred D. Taylor, *Roll of Thunder, Hear My Cry*

## Activity 2: Paragraphs

1.  Add detail to the paragraph below by writing an adverb clause at the caret.

2.  Select from the italicized words to begin your adverb clauses:
    When did it happen? (*as, when, while, before, after, until*)
    Why did it happen? (*because, since*)
    Under what conditions? (*if, although*)

**PARAGRAPH TO EXPAND** ————————————————————————————————

(1) Once on our summer vacation trip across the southwest, ^, my dad pulled the van under an overpass to wait for the storm to die down. (2) ^, my little brother began to cry. (3) Mom got out his security blanket, and, ^, she made a kind of nest for him to take a nap. (4) The van , ^, started to shake a little. (5) Suddenly the storm, subsided ^. (6) ^, the sun came out, and the storm left as fast as it had come.

## Practice 1: Identifying

The sentences below are from one of America's best-loved children's books, *Charlotte's Web*. As you do this practice, you'll notice how author E. B. White writes his sentences, a large part of his writing style. In the next practice, you'll write sentences of your own imitating E. B. White, so you'll be writing the same way as a famous author!

Each sentence in this practice contains skills taught earlier. Using the abbreviations, identify the underlined skills. If you need to review the skill, the page numbers are in parentheses.

**Phrases**                                   **Review These Pages**

AP   =   appositive phrase              (pages 34–49)

CV   =   compound verb               (pages 66–81)

P     =   present participial phrase    (pages 50–65)

PREP=   prepositional phrase          (pages 18–33)

**Clauses**

ADJC = adjective clause              (pages 82–97)
ADVC= adverb clause                 (pages 98–113)

**EXAMPLE** ——————————————————————————

**Sentence:**

(A) <u>As Wilbur came out of the crate</u>, the crowd (B) <u>clapped and cheered</u>.

E. B. White, *Charlotte's Web*

**Answers:**

(A)—ADVC (adverb clause)
(B)—CV (compound verb)

**Group 1:**

1. (A) <u>Into the night</u>, (B) <u>while the other creatures slept</u>, Charlotte worked on her web.

2. (A) <u>Underneath her rather bold and cruel exterior</u>, she (B) <u>had a kind heart and was to prove loyal and true to the very end</u>.

3. Fern just (A) <u>sat and stared out of the window</u>, (B) <u>thinking what a blissful world it was and how lucky she was to have entire charge of a pig</u>.

4. There, (A) <u>inside the carton</u>, was the newborn pig, (B) <u>a cute mound of pink, soft flesh</u>.

5. (A) <u>When Mr. Zuckerman reached the pigpen</u>, he (B) <u>climbed over the fence and poured the slops into the trough</u>.

**Group 2:**

6. (A) <u>In the distance</u>, fireworks began going off, (B) <u>scattering fiery balls in the sky</u>.

7. Templeton, (A) <u>who saved string</u>, (B) <u>crept down into his rat hole, pushed the goose egg out of the way, and returned with an old piece of dirty white string</u>.

8. Sometimes, (A) <u>on these journeys</u>, Wilbur the pig would get tired. and Fern would (B) <u>pick him up and put him in the carriage alongside the doll</u>.

9. Lurvy, (A) <u>who wasn't particularly interested in beauty</u>, noticed the web (B) <u>when he came with the pig's breakfast</u>.

10. The barn was pleasantly warm in winter (A) <u>when the animals spent most of their time indoors</u>, and it was pleasantly cool in summer (B) <u>when the big doors stood wide open in the breeze</u>.

**Group 3:**

11. (A) <u>Although Wilbur the pig loved the spider's children and grandchildren dearly</u>, none of the new spiders ever, (B) <u>in his heart</u>, quite took Charlotte's place.

12. The horses, (A) <u>in their stalls in the barn</u>, pricked up their ears (B) <u>when they heard the goose hollering</u>.

13. Charlotte the spider (A) <u>grabbed the fly, threw a few jets of silk around it, and rolled it over and over</u>, (B) <u>wrapping it so that it couldn't move</u>.

14. That pig next door, (A) <u>the one that calls himself Uncle</u>, had a blue tag (B) <u>on the front of his pen</u>.

15. The spider's web (A) <u>glistened in the light and made a pattern of loveliness and mystery</u>, (B) <u>like a delicate veil</u>.

**Group 4:**

16. Lurvy, (A) <u>the hired hand</u>, (B) <u>heard the noise and came up from the asparagus patch</u>, (C) <u>the place where he was pulling weeds</u>.

17. (A) <u>When the rotten egg broke</u>, (B) <u>with its horrible smell</u>, Templeton, (C) <u>who had been resting in his home</u>, scuttled away into the barn.

18. Wilbur the pig (A) <u>walked to the trough and took a long drink of slops</u>, (B) <u>sucking in the milk hungrily</u> and (C) <u>chewing the popover</u>.

19. (A) <u>In the cool of the evening</u>, (B) <u>when the shadows darkened the Fair Grounds</u>, Templeton the Rat (C) <u>crept from the cage and looked around</u>.

20. (A) <u>With her broad bill</u>, the goose pushed the rotten egg out of the nest, (B) <u>while the entire company watched in disgust</u> (C) <u>as the rat rolled it away to eat</u>, and even Wilbur, (D) <u>who could eat almost anything</u>, was appalled.

© 2000 by Don and Jenny Killgallon from *Sentence Composing for Elementary School*. Portsmouth, NH: Heinemann.

# Practice 2: Imitating

For each model sentence, write the letter of its imitation. Then write your own imitation of the same model.

## Group 1: Models

1. Into the night, while the other creatures slept, Charlotte worked on her web.

2. Underneath her rather bold and cruel exterior, she had a kind heart and was to prove loyal and true to the very end.

3. Fern just sat and stared out of the window, thinking what a blissful world it was and how lucky she was to have entire charge of a pig.

4. There, inside the carton, was the newborn pig, a cute mound of pink, soft flesh.

5. When Mr. Zuckerman reached the pigpen, he climbed over the fence and poured the slops into the trough.

## Group 1: Imitations

A. Now, on her neck, hung her favorite necklace, a locket in gold and silver.

B. When the clouds filled the sky, the children stayed inside and played the games kept in the cupboard.

C. Charles once stood and looked over the property, wondering how this farm would prosper and if he could work to make it worth his effort during the year.

D. Inside his usually messy and disorganized room, Willy kept a snail collection and was able to find specimens and snail shells at a moment's notice.

E. In the forest, when the sudden storm began, the fox scampered toward the cave.

## Group 2: Models

6. In the distance, fireworks began going off, scattering fiery balls in the sky.

7. Templeton, who saved string, crept down into his rat hole, pushed the goose egg out of the way, and returned with an old piece of dirty white string.

8. Sometimes, on these journeys, Wilbur the pig would get tired, and Fern would pick him up and put him in the carriage alongside the doll.

9. Lurvy, who wasn't particularly interested in beauty, noticed the web when he came with the pig's breakfast.

10. The barn was pleasantly warm in winter when the animals spent most of their time indoors, and it was pleasantly cool in summer when the big doors stood wide open in the breeze.

## Group 2: Imitations

F. Occasionally, on vacation days, Joe the gardener would stay home, and his wife would cook him breakfast and leave him in the hammock under the oak tree.

G. After the trial, reporters started gathering, asking hard questions of the witnesses.

H. Smith, who knew nothing at all about plumbing, called a professional when he discovered the broken dishwasher.

I. The rabbit, who nibbled grass, hopped into the garden, brushed the fronds with his ears, and looked for a patch of ground with fresh little weeds.

J. The days were wonderfully long in summer when the sun didn't set until late, and they were increasingly short in winter when the full moon rose earlier in the sky.

© 2000 by Don and Jenny Killgallon from *Sentence Composing for Elementary School*. Portsmouth, NH: Heinemann.

## Group 3: Models

11. Although Wilbur the pig loved the spider's children and grandchildren dearly, none of the new spiders ever, in his heart, quite took Charlotte's place.

12. The horses, in their stalls in the barn, pricked up their ears when they heard the goose hollering.

13. Charlotte the spider grabbed the fly, threw a few jets of silk around it, and rolled it over and over, wrapping it so that it couldn't move.

14. That pig next door, the one that calls himself Uncle, had a blue tag on the front of his pen.

15. The spider's web glistened in the light and made a pattern of loveliness and mystery, like a delicate veil.

## Group 3: Imitations

K. Our neighbor, on the sidewalk out front, picked up the trash when she heard the wind howling.

L. The bird outside the window, the blue jay that came every day, had lovely feathers on the tip of each wing.

M. Although Willie the inventor made new gadgets and gizmos annually, most of the new inventions, in his opinion, never matched his earlier creativity.

N. Baby Teagan's face smoothed in his sleep and showed a state of peacefulness and contentment, like a resting cherub.

O. Sandy the spy took the rope, wrapped some tape around it, and pulled it further and further, holding it so that it wouldn't drop.

## Group 4: Models

16. Lurvy, the hired hand, heard the noise and came up from the asparagus patch, the place where he was pulling weeds.

17. When the rotten egg broke, with its horrible smell, Templeton, who had been resting in his home, scuttled away into the barn.

18. Wilbur the pig walked to the trough and took a long drink of slops, sucking in the milk hungrily and chewing the popover.

19. In the cool of the evening, when the shadows darkened the Fair Grounds, Templeton the Rat crept from the cage and looked around.

20. With her broad bill, the goose pushed the rotten egg out of the nest, while the entire company watched in disgust as the rat rolled it away to eat, and even Wilbur, who could eat almost anything, was appalled.

## Group 4: Imitations

P.  After the game was won, in a heart-stopping overtime, the coach, who had been screaming to his players, settled quietly onto the bench.

Q.  At the break of day, after the sun rose over the horizon, Lex the fox returned to his den and went to sleep.

R.  Max the detective picked up the scarf and took a small corner of material, cutting the silk carefully and discovering a clue.

S.  During the unannounced fire drill, the principal stood at the front door, while all of the children left the building as the firemen arrived to investigate, and the teachers, who always responded quickly, were relieved.

T.  Smithson, a friendly waiter, dished the ice cream and stepped forward to the customer, a grandmother who was treating the grandchildren.

© 2000 by Don and Jenny Killgallon from *Sentence Composing for Elementary School*. Portsmouth, NH: Heinemann.

## Practice 3: Creating

Pretend you are the author E. B. White, and your publisher wants you to write a new paragraph for *Charlotte's Web*. The paragraph will be about one of Charlotte's children, a little spider named Charlie.

First, read carefully all of the sentences from *Charlotte's Web* in the preceding practice to review E. B. White's writing style. Notice the kind of words, the details of description, the variety in sentence lengths, and especially the interesting content. Study how E. B. White uses the six skills you learned in this worktext in his sentences.

Using E. B. White's writing style from *Charlotte's Web*, write your paragraph about something Charlie the Spider does. Choose something that would take a spider only a few minutes to do—catch a fly, climb up a plant, glide across a web, etc. Be sure to include in various positions the six skills covered in this worktext: appositive phrase, prepositional phrase, participial phrase, compound verb, adjective clause, adverb clause.

Write your paragraph so well that your readers will think it was written by the famous author of *Charlotte's Web*!

### Use This Checklist to Plan and Write Your Paragraph:

☐ Jot down ideas you want to include in your paragraph. (***pre-writing***)

☐ Write a draft of your paragraph. (***drafting***)

☐ Show it to students in your class for suggestions. (***peer response***)

☐ Follow good suggestions from peers to revise your paragraph. (***revising***)

☐ Correct misspellings, and errors in grammar and punctuation. (***editing***)

☐ Prepare a neat and attractive final copy. (***publishing***)

**Becoming a Writer**

Here are the last two sentences of *Charlotte's Web*, which identify the two excellent characteristics of Charlotte the Spider who saves the life of her friend Wilbur the Pig through her writing:

"It is not often that someone comes along who is a true friend and a good writer. Charlotte was both."

We hope that you have already learned
to be a true friend,
and that this book has helped you
to become a good writer!

Drawing by Don Killgallon

## Learning Sentence Imitating

**Practice 1** (page 2)
1. b
2. a
3. b
4. b
5. a

**Practice 2** (page 4)
1. Now Harriet nodded / and became interested, / with the Internet on her screen, / and examined the web site thoroughly.
2. Stories of courage, / stories of suspense, / stories of adventure and romance / remained in the child's memory.
3. Frying his body all day, / Jacob Johnson / got a horrible sunburn by afternoon / because the cheap suntan lotion from his brother / became a thin liquid / and dripped into the sand.
4. All kinds of vegetables, / from celery to fresh tomatoes, / were laughing or dancing or playing / in the salad bowl, / and the salad dressing / that had been as quiet and unnoticed as the bowl itself, / suddenly giggled with glee.

**Practice 3** (page 6)
1. In the final inning, / Juan caught the home run ball / that won the game.
2. Our discovery was amazing, / a treasure chest of expensive-appearing, / golden dazzling jewels.
3. A droid slid, / bent, / and fell, / and the Jedi warrior / climbed down the hill / and into the desert, / where the droid lay broken.

**Practice 4** (page 8)
1. While the weatherman gave the forecast for blue, blue skies, the weather turned nasty.
2. As the tiger chased Tarzan with fast, fast, strides, the gorillas became worried.
3. After the daffodils appeared in spring, Grandma got out her gardening tools and worked outdoors, delighted.
4. Because the puppy whimpered at night, Sandy rose from the bed and went downstairs, concerned.

**Practice 5** (page 10)
1. Baby chimpanzees, tumbling over each other, were playing tug-of-war with a banana.
2. The horses rounded the corner of the track and raced back toward the starting gate.
3. The high school students, renewing the school's agricultural field, used the tractor to give the soil a good tilling.
4. Lions and tigers and bears roamed through the forest in the frightful land of Dorothy's imagination, prowling the territory they had traveled searching for a fresh victim.

**Practice 6** (page 12)
1. She had a jump rope, an exercise tool her doctor wanted her to use when she was strengthening her legs.
2. Ralph had one brother, a neat kid Ralph's friends liked when they played baseball.
3. Hidden in a cave near the castle on the mountain was a crystal ball, a remarkable crystal ball which showed a fantasy world in color.
4. Once at the beach by our house on the cliff appeared a surfer, an amazingly old surfer who had a touch of eternal youth.

**Practice 7** (page 14)
1. When the train was very late, passengers were usually easy to spot in the restaurant.
2. Nearby, the exhibits of computers and printers filled with crowds because the sale prices lowered further.
3. Our dog dragged a big bone in its jaws, jumped the little fence, dropped the bone, and panted.

4. In the warm seashore air, seagulls flocked toward the food of wasteful residents and tourists, lunched on leftovers on beaches, picked crumbs from the sand, and ate garbage.

## Using Prepositional Phrases

### Practice 1 (page 18)

1. The horses, <u>in their stalls in the barn</u>, pricked up their ears when they heard the goose hollering.
2. <u>Inside Mrs. O'Brien's kitchen</u>, pies were baking in the oven.
3. Their path wound, in and out, <u>through the scrub</u>, <u>around palmetto clumps</u>, <u>over trunks of fallen trees</u>, <u>under dwarf pines and oaks</u>.
4. <u>To the west</u>, <u>through the trees</u>, he could see that the sun had melted into the horizon, but to the east the sky looked dark and bruised.
5. Jonas, <u>from his place in the balcony</u>, searched the auditorium for a glimpse of his father.
6. I saw the three Sadler kids, <u>in shorts and sleeveless T-shirts</u>, walking barefoot along the shore.

### Practice 2 (page 20)

1. <u>With the flavor of ham and biscuit in his mouth</u>, the boy felt good.
2. <u>Over the river</u> and <u>through the woods</u>, <u>to Grandmother's house</u> we go.
3. The curtains, <u>like her bed cover</u>, were faded and limp.
4. <u>In the moonlight</u>, Sophie caught a glimpse <u>of an enormous long wide wrinkly face</u> <u>with the most enormous ears</u>.
5. <u>For two nights and days</u>, imprisoned <u>in his crate</u>, Buck neither ate nor drank.
6. <u>By the end of the class</u>, Harry, <u>like everyone else</u>, was sweaty, aching, and covered <u>in earth</u>.

### Practice 3 (page 22)

1. On the whole enormous prairie, there was no sign that any other human being had ever been there.
2. The Monster, at the first motion, lunged forward with a terrible scream.
3. In the pine woods, along a deserted logging road, the boy and the dog came to a small open space where there had once been a log ramp.
4. With one quick movement, the boy had picked up the Indian by the waist between his thumb and forefinger.
5. Then they came, up the street and around the house.
6. In an explosion of dirt and pebbles, the pig burst from under the fence, heaving Taran into the air.

### Practice 4 (page 24)

1. <u>In a surprisingly short time</u>, he grew to recognize individual fish and to know where to find them.
2. <u>On the way</u> to school, Claire's shoes filled <u>with snow</u>.
3. <u>In his dream</u>, he stood <u>in front</u> of that very cafe, dressed only <u>in his underwear</u>.
4. <u>With an earsplitting bang</u> of metal <u>on wood</u>, they hit the thick tree trunk and dropped <u>to the ground</u> <u>with a heavy jolt</u>.

### Practice 5 (page 26)

1. On the table, there were mounds and mounds of walnuts, and the squirrels were working away like mad, shelling the walnuts at a tremendous speed.
2. The giant peach, with the sunlight glinting on its side, was like a massive golden ball sailing upon a silver sea.
3. On a night when the moon gazed down like an evil eye, the young prince appeared in Jemmy's chamber.
4. The feast finished with an entertainment provided by the Hogwarts ghosts popping out of the walls and tables to do a bit of formation gliding.

5. On the shores of Chincoteague, the people pressed forward, their faces strained to stillness as they watched Assateague Beach.
6. Then, like a glow of warmth in the chill, he felt the comforting knowledge of wild creatures near.
7. Through the glass in the door on the dryer, they watched their assorted clothing spill and splash over and over and around and around.
8. At the foot of the attic stairs, she stood still and listened.
9. With some difficulty, and with some stings from nettles and sticks from thorns, they struggled out of the thicket.
10. On the far side of the camping ground, just where the trees began, they saw the Lion slowly walking away from them into the wood.

### Practice 6 (page 28)

1. Right beside the closed door, the cat meowed and scratched, as if it were frightened.
2. Just outside the darkened classroom, children scampered and played as if they were vacationing.
3. Around the edges of the garden, they created a border and planted flowers along the row of day lilies.
4. On the top of his dresser, Jake placed his trophy and remembered his victory against the boy from his school.

### Practice 7 (page 30)

1. After the end of the birthday party, another present arrived at her house.
2. On the floor, beside the shoes and the socks, sat the magazine.
3. Down the long hall, into the crowded room, into the snaking, twisting line for the tickets, the man brought his son, whose nervous anticipation bubbled over from excitement as they waited.
4. The rain made her think of summer, of grass and honeysuckle and tomatoes, of flowers in her backyard garden, of the chirp of nesting birds' voices, singing their lovely songs of the season.

## Using Appositive Phrases

### Practice 1 (page 34)

1. Nobody was around but Snowball, <u>the white cat belonging to Mrs. Little</u>.
2. One of the pups came slowly toward me, <u>a round ball of fur that I could have held in my hand</u>.
3. <u>An avid biker</u>, Andrew has made several bicycle tours through Europe.
4. A tear, <u>a real tear</u>, trickled down his shabby velvet nose and fell to the ground.
5. It was a runt, <u>a piglet born for some reason far smaller and weaker than its brothers and sisters</u>.
6. Inside was a small white metal cupboard with a mirror in the door, <u>the kind you see over the basin in old-fashioned bathrooms</u>.

### Practice 2 (page 36)

1. This was a deer mouse, <u>a little creature with big eyes and long hind legs like a miniature kangaroo</u>.
2. Mike Mulligan had a steam shovel, <u>a beautiful red steam shovel</u>.
3. Earth, <u>our little blue and green planet with the fluffy white clouds and all</u>, is under attack.
4. On the fifth day, <u>the day before Laurie's return to London</u>, they went together to the riverbank.
5. Every year, Harry was left behind with Mrs. Figg, <u>a mad old lady who lived two streets away</u>.
6. He remembered a chipmunk he had as a small boy, <u>a pet that came when he called and ate in his hand</u>.

### Practice 3 (page 38)

1. Moana, the Sea God, was reaching up for them, seeking to draw them down to his dark heart.
2. Curtis and Doug, two of Jeff's friends, came out of Mrs. Sharp's class.
3. As far back as the 1960's, Dr. John Lilly, the first scientist to attempt communication with dolphins, had suggested ways in which they might cooperate with man.

4. Buck did not read the newspapers, and he did not know that Manuel, one of the gardener's helpers, was an undesirable acquaintance.
5. Grey damp would be around them, and the sun, a copper penny, would fade away.
6. The scrub, that big wild stretch of dry and sandy land where scrub oaks, scrub pines, and palmettos grew, was an unexplored wilderness, always beckoning the children.

## Practice 4 (page 40)

1. One of them, <u>a tan Jersey named Blind Tillie</u>, was Cold Sassy's champion milk producer.
2. Henry, <u>the elevator operator</u>, is always making jokes about me and Sheila.
3. Once they even went to St. Louis, <u>a city far away from here</u>, just to dance.
4. The reason for this was that the toothpaste factory, <u>the place where Mr. Bucket worked</u>, suddenly went bust and had to close down.
5. Beside the hedgerow, she met Straw, <u>the horse who was in pain from a toothache</u>.
6. She chose James, the second youngest of their three younger brothers.

## Practice 5 (page 42)

1. Wilbur planned to have a talk with Templeton, the rat that lived under his trough.
2. Once upon a time there was a bat, a little brown bat, the color of coffee with cream in it.
3. The ponies were scrambling up the beach, the long, sandy island which shelters the tidewater country of Virginia and Maryland.
4. They all saw it this time, a whiskered face which had looked out at them from behind a tree.
5. It was a pitiful sight, the three of us in our overcoats and boots, standing among the dead stalks of winter.
6. Suddenly they were aware of someone coming toward them, a tall man in rough clothes with a musket over his shoulder.
7. On the fifth day, the day before Laurie's return to London, they went together to the riverbank.
8. He felt the young man's surge of joy at seeing his brother alive, the brother he had thought dead and buried in a forgotten part of the forest.
9. Tom Grieves, the handyman who had to clean up the cage, named the birds Peter Soil and Maggie Mess.
10. He came so close she could see on his head a few last straggly pinfeathers, the feathers that adorned him as a baby.

## Practice 6 (page 44)

1. Susan picked up her favorite book, a fantasy with incredible characters.
2. Mr. Short looked over his current project, a painting of his son.
3. The child stumbled, a stumble so awkward that her mother tried to lift her and help her.
4. The lightning flashed, a flash so bright that the sky seemed to light up the ground and frame it.

## Practice 7 (page 46)

1. The third base player followed the ball closely, a fly ball in her area now.
2. The cable company featured a new channel with lots of great movies, pretty much an assortment of titles with action and suspense.
3. The baby, a really frisky toddler, walked around in her diapers, waddling like a duck.
4. Angie went to the store in the mall that sold electronics products, the mall where stores tried to sell things only at discount prices.

## Using Participial Phrases

## Practice 1 (page 50)

1. Suddenly the shark soared up out of the water in a fountain of spray, <u>turning as it fell</u>.
2. The children, <u>shouting and screaming</u>, came charging back into their homeroom.

3. The ponies rolled in the wiry grass, <u>letting out great whinnies of happiness</u>.
4. The fly in the spider web was beating its wings furiously, <u>trying to break loose and free itself</u>.
5. <u>Thinking maybe I was dreaming</u>, I closed my eyes again.
6. I dream I'm flying over a sandy beach in the early morning, <u>touching the leaves of the trees as I fly by</u>.

## Practice 2 (page 52)

1. <u>Arriving at the used-up haystack</u>, the boy leaned against the barbed wire fence.
2. The snow swirled, <u>blurring his vision</u>.
3. A cloud shadow, <u>drifting the breadth of Trial Valley</u>, spread across the inscrutable face of Old Joshua.
4. <u>Lying back in the soft hay</u>, I folded my hands behind my head, closed my eyes, and let my mind wander back over the two long years.
5. Billy ate it offhand, sideways, <u>reading a comic book</u>.
6. <u>Returning to the lab to put a bucket of water on the stove for dish washing</u>, she noticed that Mitch was not at the computer, although it was turned on.

## Practice 3 (page 54)

1. There is Sadako, standing on top of a granite mountain of paradise.
2. Still holding him by the ears, the Trunchbull lowered him back into his chair beside the desk.
3. He was standing very still, holding it tightly with both hands while the crowd pushed and shouted all around him.
4. That afternoon, a big man came and pried off the drain cover, grunting as he worked.
5. She lay very still with her eyes closed, letting herself awaken slowly.
6. Standing in the clear sunshine, the prince breathed in the sweet, fresh air.

## Practice 4 (page 56)

1. Charles Wallace braced, <u>trying to tighten the grip of his legs about the unicorn's broad neck</u>.
2. The children crowded in, <u>stamping their bare feet on the floor to shake the dust off</u>.
3. Now when a buyer came to look at the colts, Maureen did not run to her room as she used to do, <u>pressing her face in the feather bed to stifle her sobs</u>.
4. The White Witch rose and went out, <u>ordering Edmund to go with her</u>.
5. Matilda, <u>nestling in her usual chair</u>, was watching this performance over the rim of her book with some interest.
6. Faster and faster the Polar Express ran along, <u>rolling over peaks and through valleys like a car on a roller coaster</u>.

## Practice 5 (page 58)

1. As they swung on the turn, the sled went over, spilling half its load through the loose lashings.
2. Dad, sitting on the edge of the porch, leaned forward so he could see.
3. Coming silently down the tunnel, she could hear them talking in the room below, and she paused a moment to eavesdrop on their conversation.
4. The wind blew in fierce gusts as we left the village, stinging our faces with sand.
5. The next day after school, Jess went down and got the lumber he needed, carrying it a couple of boards at a time to the creek bank.
6. The sound came from the end of one corridor, and I fumbled along, peering into each cage to try to see a tiger cat in a shadowy hole.
7. She just sat and stared out of the window, thinking what a blissful world it was and how lucky she was to have entire charge of a pig.
8. Sitting so close to the desk, I could see that the covers of the books were badly worn.
9. Ben got down on his hands and knees and eased his body over the edge of the cliff, slowing the swing downward with his legs and knees rather than with his sore feet.
10. The frightening sound filled the forest, echoing through the trees.

**Practice 6** (page 60)

1. She waited very small and quiet and timid, twisting the scarf nervously on her lap.
2. He flew very high and straight and true, moving swiftly over the stark landscape.
3. Standing there on the court, Burt started to dribble the ball up and down on the foul line.
4. Thinking seriously about her friend, she began to remember the laughter and tears over their many adventures.

**Practice 7** (page 62)

1. His dog jumped around him excitedly, begging for a treat.
2. Opening the present, she had a smile on her face, a well-pleased clear expression of delight.
3. Sunshine, dazzling and golden, shone like yellow watercolors on the fresh morning horizon.
4. Maybe one of the dogs, straying, saw in the woods a rabbit, emerging from its warren.

## Using Compound Verbs

**Practice 1** (page 66)

1. Birdie <u>wiped off the girl's tears</u>, <u>took her to the back porch</u>, and <u>washed her face in the washbasin</u>.
2. The milk lady <u>fished two mugs out of a tub of water</u>, <u>sat on a stool</u>, and <u>began to milk the cow directly into the mugs</u>.
3. A burning limb <u>fell into the pit</u>, <u>struck the water</u>, <u>hissed like a snake</u>, and <u>went out</u>.
4. He <u>climbed up a great big tall heaping mountain of snow</u> and <u>slid all the way down</u>.
5. Then I <u>swung my chopping ax high</u> and <u>wheeled</u>, aiming to cave in the bear's head with the first lick.
6. The spotted twin cats, Romulus and Remus, <u>crawled through the kitchen window</u>, and <u>returned with a large paper package of fish</u>.

**Practice 2** (page 68)

1. Ramona <u>scowled</u> and <u>slid down in her chair</u>.
2. They <u>took him away</u> and <u>shut him in a prison</u>.
3. The large woman <u>simply turned around</u> and <u>kicked him right square in his blue-jeaned sitter</u>.
4. They <u>climbed narrow steps</u> and <u>opened creaking doors to three small rooms with beds under dust covers</u>.
5. I <u>let out a terrified howl</u>, <u>scrambled to my feet</u>, and <u>lurched away from his bony, outstretched hand</u>.
6. He <u>nose-dived into the grass</u>, <u>turned a somersault</u>, <u>rolled over a few times on the steep slope</u>, and <u>landed on the next ant heap, six feet away</u>.

**Practice 3** (page 70)

1. With these words, the Witch fell down into a melted shapeless mass and began to spread over the kitchen floor.
2. Very quietly, the two girls groped their way among the other sleepers and crept out of the tent.
3. Garlands of flowers hung from every house and shop and carpeted the streets.
4. Sara curled herself up in the window-seat, opened a book, and began to read.
5. Then Beezus came into the kitchen through the back door, dropped her books on the table, and flopped down on a chair a gusty sigh.
6. The king gripped the arms of the chair, closed his eyes, clenched his teeth, and sweated.

**Practice 4** (page 72)

1 The Monkeys <u>flew the Tinman high in the air</u> and <u>dropped him on sharp rocks</u>.
2. Leslie <u>whirled</u> and <u>began to duel the imaginary foe</u>.
3. She <u>took a deep breath</u>, <u>then smiled</u>, and <u>patted the rabbit on its head</u>.
4. She <u>grabbed the little gold chain</u>, <u>yanked with all her strength</u>, and <u>broke it</u>.
5. She <u>got out of bed</u>, <u>pushed her feet into furry slippers</u>, and <u>went downstairs</u>.
6. The dog <u>escorted the Judge's daughters on rambles</u>, <u>carried the Judge's grandsons on his back</u>, and, on wintry nights, <u>lay at the Judge's feet before the roaring fire</u>.

**Practice 5** (page 74)

1. He fell with his leg twisted under him and could hear the crack of bone.
2. He tumbled upside down and reached up the tree trunk with his feet.
3. Suddenly, a slim white cat sped through the grass, dashed up the maple tree, and began to sing.
4. Now and again strangers came, gave money to the man in the red sweater, and took one or more dogs away.
5. Bradley scribbled, cut up bits of paper, and taped things together.
6. At that moment, Patsy raced in, threw herself at the bed, snatched a blanket, and made off with it.
7. Mrs. Jones stopped, jerked him around in front of her, put a half-nelson about his neck, and continued to drag him up the street.
8. The Giant crept downstairs and opened the front door quite softly and went out into the garden.
9. The boy put the dog's dish under the porch, closed the door, pushed the night latch, sat down behind the stove, and began to eat his supper.
10. He cut poles and slung his tarp for a roof, quickly laid up stones for a fireplace, gathered wood, and built a fire.

**Practice 6** (page 76)

1. He pulled over, got out his license, and put it out on the dashboard.
2. She listened carefully, took out her notebook, and wrote it all down on one page.
3. Frank anchored the boat, moved it out of the sun, and heard it slap the water and sea grass in rhythm.
4. Susan fed Buttercup, moved her toward the barn, and saw the cow navigate the barnyard and stall doors with impatience.

**Practice 7** (page 78)

1. The teacher went once again to the board, drew the map, and questioned the class about the correct location.
2. The ladybug crawled out, stood quietly inside the grass of the lawn, then flew unexpectedly, and disappeared quickly.
3. The sun came up with a burst of color, covered the horizon with light, and glowed, filling the sky with warmth, spilling across the fields of clover.
4. The referee blew his whistle, bent down to retrieve the ball, raised his voice with authority, and quickly negotiated.

## Using Adjective Clauses

**Practice 1** (page 82)

1. Gwydion, <u>whose eyes were everywhere at once</u>, caught sight of them instantly.
2. Sara opened the paper bag and took out one of the hot buns, <u>which had already warmed her own cold hands a little</u>.
3. Ramo was standing on one foot and then the other, watching the ship coming, <u>which he did not know was a ship because he had never seen one</u>.
4. The old woman beside him, <u>whose arm he held</u>, was hunched over as she shuffled along in her soft slippers.
5. Heidi, <u>who had never seen so huge a cat</u>, stopped to admire her.
6. The little prince, <u>who asked me so many questions</u>, never seemed to hear the ones I asked him.

**Practice 2** (page 84)

1. Susie was a sleek, excited matron of some three hundred pounds, <u>who reared herself out of the water as they approached</u>.

2. Little Jon, <u>whose eyes were quicker than most</u>, should have seen the hole, but all his attention was on the stars.

3. There was a gate in the wall, <u>whose locks were jawbones set with sharp teeth</u>.

4. It was a dog, <u>which hopped along on three legs</u>, crying softly and holding up a front paw.

5. Sandy and Dennis, her ten-year-old twin brothers, <u>who got home from school an hour earlier than she did</u>, were disgusted.

6. Miss Crocker walked stiffly to her desk, <u>which was set on a tiny platform and piled high with bulky objects covered by a tarpaulin</u>.

## Practice 3 (page 86)

1. The great coon dog, whose rhythmic panting came through the porch floor, came from under the porch and began to whine.

2. Benny caught the boy by the shoulder before he could run to the bear, which was bawling and snapping at the chair.

3. Boysie, who slept in the kitchen, heard the door shut and came to the living room.

4. The stallion neighed encouragement to his mares, who were struggling to keep afloat, fighting the wreckage and the sea.

5. The old woman's voice was fading, and she named the gift very softly, but her daughter, who loved her greatly, was weeping and did not hear.

6. Behind her in the shadows, he could see the little boy, who must have been about his own age.

## Practice 4 (page 88)

1. He put the big blood heart, <u>which was still beating</u>, into her hands.

2. The sheep, <u>who had moved slightly away as he had come into the pasture</u>, turned now to stare at him

3. There was Crook Arm, <u>whose left arm dangled down uselessly by his side</u>, with two of his fingers missing.

4. On her way back she met the Prince, <u>who pulled up his horse and scowled at her so that she might not see the love in his eyes</u>.

5. One piece of aspirin flew out of sight under the stove, and the other piece, <u>which she got down the boy's throat with no little difficulty</u>, came up again promptly, along with the bowl of soup she had coaxed down.

6. Miss Crocker was sitting at Miss Davis's desk, staring fiercely down at Little Man, <u>who was pushing a book back upon the desk</u>.

## Practice 5 (page 90)

1. Harry was a white dog with black spots, who liked everything except getting a bath.

2. She also had to watch our three chickens, who loved to wander away from our farm.

3. Stacey, who generally overlooked T. J.'s underhanded stunts, shook his head.

4. When she couldn't stand it anymore, she kicked off the blankets and walked over to her Barbie doll, which lay on a chest of drawers.

5. Across the stalk land into the pine woods, into the climbing, brightening glow of dawn, the boy followed the dog, whose anxious pace slowed from age as they went.

6. Gwydion, who had been sitting thoughtfully at the table and turning the splintered rods back and forth in his hands, rose and spoke to the companions.

7. Nurse, who had informed him that her name was Tessie and that she came from the island of Tongs, watched approvingly while he ate a hearty meal of eggs, canned meat, and tropical fruits.

8. Her dear mamma, who had died when she was born, had been French.

9. That night he kept a fire going and sat watching for the lion, which came and prowled the nearby darkness, growling but fire-wary.

10. This leader, whose word was law among boys who defied authority for the sake of defiance, was no more than twelve or thirteen years old and looked even younger.

**Practice 6** (page 92)

1. Roland and Freddie and Chamon, who had talked themselves out of trouble, stood quietly at the back of the room.
2. Mattie and Sarah and Eve, who had reassured themselves during the storm, walked outside the shed near the barn.
3. Under the back porch and the old steps, whose planks were always rotting, the treasure had remained undiscovered.
4. Near the oak tree and the barn, whose doors were wide open, the puppies had found safety.

**Practice 7** (page 94)

1. Also the pen, which had been new, seemed broken.
2. Meg, who was reading the book, looked very closely at the utterly beautiful illustrations.
3. Slowly I copied down the popular lyric, which I listen to every day, and put it in my notebook behind the math problems.
4. He thought about his friend, who must have been a happy and healthy baby, for he was a happy and healthy boy, excited after his speech, hoping to be chosen by their classmates.

## Using Adverb Clauses

**Practice 1** (page 98)

1. <u>When they heard the fire engine</u>, the children in the school across the street couldn't keep their eyes on their lessons.
2. <u>Since my childhood feels like a story</u>, I decided to tell it that way.
3. Each night, Mother Bat would carry Stellaluna clutched to her breast <u>as she flew out to search for food</u>.
4. The first floor, <u>because it was closest to the garbage in the empty lot</u>, was where the rats lived.
5. His voice seemed sad, <u>although he was trying to be cheerful</u>.
6. <u>If he had no good clothes</u>, at least he had no place to go which required good clothes.

**Practice 2** (page 100)

1. They crossed one deep valley, then another, <u>before Gurgi halted on a ridge</u>.
2. <u>When flour was scarce</u>, the boy's mother would wrap the leftover biscuits in a clean flour sack and put them away for the next meal.
3. The penguin chicks, <u>when they began to hatch</u>, were not so handsomely marked as their mother and father.
4. <u>When the tinkling little melody began</u>, Winnie's sobbing slowed.
5. <u>As she let herself in through the gleaming white front door</u>, her father appeared in the double doors of the living room.
6. Her face, <u>when he stepped into the light</u>, was round and thick, and her eyes were like two immense eggs stuck into a white mess of bread dough.

**Practice 3** (page 102)

1. He began to dig again, driving the spade deep into the rich, black garden soil while the robin hopped about very busily employed.
2. When Miss Munchkin sent her sister, Miss Amelia, to see what the child was doing, she found she could not open the door.
3. The second box, as she moved on to it, was filled with papers.
4. As the little prince dropped off to sleep, I took him in my arms and set out walking once more.
5. She would not need a calender or a clock if she knew enough about nature.
6. When I was in elementary school, I packed by suitcase and told my mother I was going to run away.

## Practice 4 (page 104)

1. <u>While Taran struggled to his feet</u>, Gwydion seized him like a sack of meal and hauled him to Melyngar's back.
2. The bright autumn leaves stuck in her hair <u>as she twisted her head back and forth</u>.
3. <u>Although he could tell it was daylight</u>, he kept his eyes shut tight.
4. She wrapped her arms around her knees <u>as she watched a dried leaf scratch along the driveway in the autumn wind</u>.
5. <u>Before she went to sleep</u>, Sadako managed to fold only one paper crane.
6. <u>While Maggie watched</u>, the spider rolled up her web and carried the silvery ball to her hideout.

## Practice 5 (page 106)

1. When we got on the train, I felt as if everybody must be looking at me and pitying me.
2. The truck drivers, when they heard that Maxie Hammerman had been released, were furious.
3. The superintendent, Fred Snood, checked the cellar storage cages, after a passing youth hinted to him that there had been a robbery.
4. While I was resting there, sucking the juice from the cactus, I saw the big gray dog, the leader of the wild pack, in the brush above me.
5. Miss Ellis flinched at the pop of Gilly's gum but continued to talk in her calm, professional voice while Gilly picked at the bits of gum stuck in her straggly bangs and on her cheeks and chin.
6. Although each night Big Ma prepared a pot of hot soapy water for him to wash out his clothing, each day he arrived home looking as if his pants had not been washed in more than a month.
7. If his dog Marcel jumped on the furniture, Bibot was sure to teach him a lesson.
8. While Mrs. Post hurried with the little boy up the wide marble steps of the big porch, Anna's father went around to the back door of the van to take down her wheelchair.
9. Dicey was up and dressed, washed and fed, and out the door, with the day's work outlined in her head, before anyone else stirred in the silent house.
10. When your stomach is empty and your mind is full, it's hard to sleep.

## Practice 6 (page 108)

1. After Brennan opened the package, he ran into the family room and shared his new book with his siblings.
2. When Kylie ate the cookie, she removed the yucky raisins and made a pile on her napkin.
3. In early spring, when the sun was shining, all the gardeners would go to the stores in their neighborhoods, and employees would sell them mulch.
4. On Saturday mornings, if their parents were asleep, all of the children would sit on the floor of the den, and Prentice would imitate their father's behavior.

## Practice 7 (page 110)

1. When a small child cries bitter tears over a lost toy, it is like watching rains from a sudden storm.
2. When Lou the New Carrot got chosen for the salad, he waited on the counter and began thinking about the other vegetables.
3. As chairs pushed back and books of the students appeared, she saw many smiling faces.
4. As she was passing the museum, thinking about the many, many exhibits she had helped create, she was delighted to watch an excited, enthusiastic group going up the steps toward the large entrance.

## Reviewing and Creating Good Writing

**Practice 1** (page 114)

| | | | |
|---|---|---|---|
| 1. (A) PREP | (B) ADVC | | |
| 2. (A) PREP | (B) CV | | |
| 3. (A) CV | (B) P | | |
| 4. (A) PREP | (B) AP | | |
| 5. (A) ADVC | (B) CV | | |
| 6. (A) PREP | (B) P | | |
| 7. (A) ADJC | (B) CV | | |
| 8. (A) PREP | (B) CV | | |
| 9. (A) ADJC | (B) ADVC | | |
| 10. (A) ADVC | (B) ADVC | | |
| 11. (A) ADVC | (B) PREP | | |
| 12. (A) PREP | (B) ADVC | | |
| 13. (A) CV | (B) P | | |
| 14. (A) AP | (B) PREP | | |
| 15. (A) CV | (B) PREP | | |
| 16. (A) AP | (B) CV | (C) AP | |
| 17. (A) ADVC | (B) PREP | (C) ADJC | |
| 18. (A) CV | (B) P | (C) P | |
| 19. (A) PREP | (B) ADVC | (C) CV | |
| 20. (A) PREP | (B) ADVC | (C) ADVC | (D) ADJC |

**Practice 2** (page 118)

| | | | |
|---|---|---|---|
| 1. E | 6. G | 11. M | 16. T |
| 2. D | 7. I | 12. K | 17. P |
| 3. C | 8. F | 13. O | 18. R |
| 4. A | 9. H | 14. L | 19. Q |
| 5. B | 10. J | 15. N | 20. S |

© 2000 by Don and Jenn[...] [...]ool. Portsmouth, NH: Heinemann.